The Line of Least Existence
and Other Plays

ALSO BY ROSALYN DREXLER

I AM THE BEAUTIFUL STRANGER

The Line of Least Existence and *Other Plays*

Home Movies

The Investigation

Hot Buttered Roll

Softly, and Consider the Nearness

The Bed Was Full

ROSALYN DREXLER

With an Introduction by Richard Gilman

 RANDOM HOUSE · NEW YORK

for RACHEL

CONTENTS

INTRODUCTION

"Don't you know that appearance is everything and style is a way of living?" a character in one of Rosalyn Drexler's plays tells another, thereby establishing a motto for all the plays in this book as well as for the rest of the good new drama that has slyly and suddenly begun to emerge in this country. A couple of flaming heresies—but only by the orthodoxies of our conventional theater—these motions of appearance being *everything,* nothing behind, nothing beneath, and of style being neither instrument nor adornment but actual substance, the thing itself. Once you find yourself looking behind the appearance of a play, or of any work of art, to discover what it's *really* about, or thinking of style as a means of expressing something besides itself, some purported body of truth previously holed up somewhere, you may come into all sorts of windfalls, but you can be sure they won't be aesthetic ones.

There aren't any truths about human life that can be extrapolated like lecture titles from Rosalyn Drexler's work. All the truths she has to offer are contained in the appearance of her plays, in her style—the words and gestures she selects, the way her imagination chooses to live publicly. Imagination equals style equals play; until we learn that this is so, we are going to go on hunting like demented ferrets for the truth underneath the surfaces of the plays we see, nosing, snuffling, rooting around, and never experiencing what is there to be experienced. A rule of thumb: any play whose major energies go into hinting at deeper and greater truths than its surface displays is a bad play—no exceptions. Most Broadway dramas are, of course, of this kind.

Rosalyn Drexler's plays suggest, more than anything else, the early Marx Brothers. Wayward, full of lip, fantastic yet anchored in domesticity, they work at reordering all those matter-of-fact details, from the date on the calendar to the necessity of putting on one shoe after another, which obstruct us in our pursuit of significant whim and appetite. They are also Marxian in many of their characters' lordly self-contempt, which is the greatest advantage we can establish over others. The following exchange is pure Groucho:

"If I wasn't so depressed I couldn't stand you for two seconds. You're not my type."

"I'm not my type either. I don't relish the picture I present, but so what?"

As is this one-liner:

"Someday I'm going to start something I can't finish and then you'll be proud of me."

But Rosalyn Drexler is an inhabitant of our generation, not of the thirties: here is a bit of dialogue which the Marx Brothers, with their avid-innocent sexual dispositions, might have loved to have engaged in but which the *Zeitgeist* would have prevented:

Mrs. Toolon-Fraak: "I want to know why you spend more time on the upper half of your body than you do on the lower half of mine."

Dr. Toolon-Fraak: "I didn't know you wanted a shave."

This newer vocabulary of sexuality—freer, more perverse, if you will—is only one of the elements of Mrs. Drexler's very contemporary sensibility. Like the Marx Brothers, she is interested in upsetting applecarts, but she is the beneficiary of post-Marxist techniques for upsetting a number of applecarts at once. Both language and psychology, for example, suffer a simultaneous assault on their congealed natures, their stiff claims to light-giving, in the following exchange from "The Bed Was Full":

Jordan: "See if you can't engage him in harmless kinky talk. Converse with him about matters of flagellation and Dalmation."

Jewel: "Don't you mean damnation?"

Jordan: "I say what I mean and I mean what I say—Dalmation!"

Yet Mrs. Drexler's plays aren't simply a set of brilliant verbal exercises (although that would be enough to make her an outstanding benefactress to a theater starved for language). All her dialogue issues from an imagination which has previously discovered the uses of language for new guise, for bluff, feint, decoy and red herring—all necessary properties and instrumentalities of the crucial game that goes on in most of her work. The game might be called "keep them guessing" or "never give a sucker an even break." For Mrs. Drexler's imagination holds that the world is forever trying to impose roles and indentities upon us which it is our duty and pleasure to resist and repudiate, by outwitting the identifiers and the casting directors.

None of the "characters" in her plays (with two exceptions) is interested in the "meaning" of his life or of anyone else's, in overt moral truth, in social or psychological values; none is in "lifelike" relation to the others; none has a history or a future, a place to go after the play is over. They have all been invented only in order to rush madly around, armed to the teeth with language and also with the capacity to be quick-change artists, con men and false prophets, wolves in sheep's clothing and the reverse, so that they might do nothing else than establish an atmosphere of freedom. Continually causing one another to lose footing, slipping on each other's banana peels, turning up in each other's beds, clothes, baths and mirrors, they make up new worlds of farce whose highly serious intention, as in all true examples of the genre, is to liberate us from the way things are said to be.

In none of these plays (again with one exception) is there a denouement that is in any sense convincing or for which there could not be half a dozen substitutes. Denouements, after all, are for plays which progress from a question to an answer, whereas Mrs. Drexler's movement is exactly the other way round. The exception is "The Investigation," a drama which would seem to be quite untypical in its straightforward representation of the encounter between a young sex criminal and a tough detective. Yet even here, in Mrs. Drexler's one "serious" drama, her one appropriation of the newspapers and the sociology books, the chief quality distilled is that of humor—a bitter, dark humor which has its roots in the undermining of conventional attitudes and stock responses, in the overthrow of the structure of solid meaning we erect to house what disturbs us.

For the rest, for "Home Movies," with its wondrous domestic bestiary, for "The Bed Was Full" and "Hot Buttered Roll," with their zany cabals and parodic handling of modern myths, and for the biggest and best play in this volume, "The Line of Least Existence," with its complex fabric of false action and false reaction, of masks beneath masks and gestures hiding gestures—the only thing that remains to be said is that everything is there, on the surface. Try skating on it; I guarantee it will hold you up.

The Line of Least Existence

CAST

MRS. CAROL TOLOON-FRAAK   The doctor's wife.

DR. TOLOON-FRAAK   The psychiatrist-pimp-pusher-husband.

ANDY   A hip-talking dog; the family pet.

PSCHUG   Father of Ibolya, a former patient of the doctor.

IBOLYA   Daughter of Pschug, an employee of the doctor.

FRED
ED
DAN   Three "Feds" disguised as a rock and roll group called The Feds.

VOICE ON HOUSE-PHONE   Dr. Toloon-Fraak (ventriloquist or on tape).

Act One

*The audience enters a blazingly lit theater to the gentle sound
of coughing, sneezing, weeping, laughing, nose blowing, dog barking, and soft, throaty laughter. When the audience is seated, the
lights go out and one spotlight, in which* PSCHUG *appears, is directed
center stage. During his opening speech the spot shifts and* PSCHUG
*tries to get back into it. The soft, throaty laughter mocks him and
seems to control the spot.* PSCHUG *has a microphone around his
neck; it is amplified to a deafening shout. He carries a brown paper
shopping bag.*

PSCHUG   To you fellow citizens of concern, if you are listening to
my question, I have lost a runaway daughter. I go to the authori-
ties one, two, three times. They give me papers to bring me into
jail. In this jail I have still to remember my message and am
ready to bring it to you in more amplified and true voice than
before. My daughter name is, when last seen by me, Maria
Della Ibolya. She who is five feet four inch tall and have dark
eyes, a fine nose, and full hair. On her way to masquerade party
of gang interest this is my daughter Ibolya: birth 3/23/47. Pitui-
tary five foot four inch. Eye: brown. Hair: brown. Who have in
gang position dirty immoral life since 1960. Gang interest and
mixed guilty hands. I know this case is complicate and that all
this sounds impossible, but see, all my proofs is over ten pounds
and one thousand foot recording tape minutes. (*He takes tapes
out of his shopping bag*) This is true story, to all whom it may
concern. (*We hear the sound of a dog,* ANDY, *barking*) In Greenvue Hospital, New York, ward N3, guilty Dr. Fraaks or Dr.
Toloon associate with boys three times a week and teach smoking and other etc. which done by any moral country just prostitute my daughter who when home is virgin and happy have good
moral and religion life. Proofs my daughter hand writt letters
(*He takes bundles of letters out of the bag*) from 1957 to 1960.
This terror case illegal. Illegal took my life savings money

7

$2,354.00 and fifty cents, illegal many other items, two big packages, my daughter, my personally documents disappeared. And you want light on this case? (*There is blinking light and the sound of an ambulance*) Attention competent department! White slavery traders, racketeering, kidnapping, immoral terror gang interest broke. I have prophecy gift! I sincerely have a mail address, I am Hungarian refugee and special color printer. I am willing to give every assistance to the authorities. I want real U.S. Constitution and law, not a jungle Al Capone law prevail which used even today. My daughter untrue diagnosis—schizophrenic personality disturb: signed Dr. Toloon-Fraak. And you want light on this case? (*There is a blackout*) Put you in a mental ward—here it is easy and heavy go out. And you never have justice, not believe to you! (*There is soft laughter as the scene ends*)

SCENE 2

The bedroom of the Toloon-Fraak's. MRS. FRAAK *is nervously walking back and forth. She wears a microphone around her neck. It has a long extension cord attached to it, which she swings out of her way, handling it like the train of a gown. A dog,* ANDY, *wearing dark glasses, follows her.* DR. TOLOON-FRAAK *enters from the bathroom gargling and wiping his mouth with kleenex which shreds on his face. He is half shaved, half lathered. He approaches* MRS. FRAAK *and gargles into her microphone.* DR. FRAAK *is wearing a long-jacketed, double-breasted brown striped suit.*

DR. FRAAK *(Snapping his fingers into the microphone)* Testing, testing, we're testing. I think I'm on.

MRS. FRAAK Of course you're on. What do you mean, you think you're on? I had my mike fixed last week. How loud do you want it? Go ahead, increase the volume, I'll run into the bathroom and close the door. *(She runs into the bathroom and closes the door)* Okay, say anything. I'll bet I hear you.

DR. FRAAK You forgot to give me the mike.

MRS. FRAAK What?

DR. FRAAK *(He goes to the bathroom door and opens it. He whispers)* You forgot to give me the mike.

MRS. FRAAK Oh, here it is. *(She gives it to him and puts it around his neck like a regal robing.* DR. FRAAK *goes to the end of the bedroom.* MRS. FRAAK *slams the bathroom door)* Okay, talk to me. Say something. Anything.

DR. FRAAK I'd like to apologize for being a bad lover.

MRS. FRAAK What? Make it louder!

9

DR. FRAAK (*Louder*) I'd like to apologize for being a bad lover!

MRS. FRAAK Louder!

DR. FRAAK I'd like to apologize for being a bad lover.

MRS. FRAAK I don't hear you. You don't know how to work it. Turn the volume up. Don't you know what "up" is?

DR. FRAAK (*Removing the mike, he speaks softly*) Up your ass.

MRS. FRAAK (*She comes out of the bathroom*) I heard that. If that's your message, go tell it to someone in your office, not to me. I don't want to receive a message like that. I want babies.

DR. FRAAK Who's stopping you?

MRS. FRAAK I don't know. When it comes down to it, I don't know. I try and I try. Every day I try.

ANDY Woof, woof!

DR. FRAAK Every marriage has its sadness, has its gladness, has its badness. (*His mood changes to energetic cheerfulness*) And now I must finish shaving.
       (*He goes into the bathroom*)

MRS. FRAAK (*Singing into the mike*)
       My love for you is très tragique,
       I know at last that you're a creep.
       If I don't get a lover soon,
       I'll turn into a dried-out prune.

ANDY Great woofy delivery. I'd like to be your manager.

MRS. FRAAK (*To* ANDY) Something's going on with the doctor. I think something's going on with him. Andy, have you noticed anything different about your master lately?

ANDY Offhand, I'd say it's his lack of hair. He isn't hairy enough. He shaves too often and he doesn't know how to bark out orders. He's too paternal.

MRS. FRAAK That's nothing new. I mean, you're not telling me something I don't know. But haven't you watched him coming and going late at night, muttering, searching through his pockets for small change and then going out to a public phone booth to make his calls when he has three phones here at home and four at the office!

ANDY It isn't my place to check on him. I'd be out of my class entirely. I'm here for a number of reasons: One, to be an object of displaced affection. Two, to guard your life and property. Three—I haven't figured three out yet.

MRS. FRAAK You are my only confidant, Andy. I can tell you anything. That's the third reason.

ANDY (*Proudly*) Woof, woof! I'm the soul of canine discretion.

MRS. FRAAK In a world of dog-eat-dog, you prefer to sharpen your teeth on my kibbles, don't you, darling? I trust you, I love you. Come here, Andy. (*She kisses the air*) Here Andy, here doggy, doggy. (*Whistles*) That's a friendly dog. That's a loving Andy. Come give Mommy your paw.
    (ANDY *frisks around happily before he patters over to* MRS. FRAAK *and sweetly puts a paw in her lap. She is seated on the bed. He gazes into her eyes. She gazes into his*)

MRS. FRAAK Give Mommy a nice wet kiss. Wash Mommy's face.

ANDY Just a minute. I have to woof off my shades. (ANDY *whips off his glasses*) Mistress, you're even woofier up close than when seen through the smoky lenses of my world. (MRS. FRAAK *leans over to put out a bedside lamp*) No, don't do that. The glare of light has a fierce intensity to it that excites my growling groin. Leave it be on.

MRS. FRAAK (*Resuming her former position*) But my pupils are getting smaller every minute and my eyes look so much more beautiful when they expand and round out and darken like a pool of liver.

ANDY (*Disgusted*) Like a pool of cat food. That would be the end of your eyes.

MRS. FRAAK (*Shoving him away; then singing*)
The end of my eyes,
The end of your sighs,
The end of your lies,
The last, last goodbyes,
Goodbye-Goodbye-Goodbye!

DR. FRAAK (*Coming out of the bathroom*) Hello. Hello, you adorable singer. I'm the only one in the world who appreciates your singing. I think it's divine. Sing on! (ANDY *frisks around the doctor.* DR. FRAAK *kicks* ANDY *away.* ANDY *goes to* MRS. FRAAK *and tries to leap into her lap*) Scram, you're shedding on my wife. Now dear, sing on!
     (*He waves an imaginary baton.* MRS. FRAAK *begins tentatively*)

MRS. FRAAK (*Singing*)
The end of my eyes,

DR. FRAAK (*Singing*)
Please salt the french-fries.

MRS. FRAAK
The end of your sighs.

DR. FRAAK
Just twenty cents buys

MRS. FRAAK
The last of your lies.

DR. FRAAK
Don't charge for the flies.

MRS. FRAAK
The last, last goodbyes.

DR. FRAAK
Let's throw a few pies.

BOTH
Goodbye, goodbye, goodbye.

ANDY
Woof, woof, woof.
  (DR. FRAAK *goes back into the bathroom*)

MRS. FRAAK He may be a doctor, but he can't carry a tune, and he doesn't want me to carry a baby, and he's always falling in love with his patients. I can't imagine what he needs me for.

ANDY He's sentimental.

MRS. FRAAK I think he's using me as a front. Have you ever thought of biting him?

ANDY No.

MRS. FRAAK (*Petulantly*) Why not!

ANDY He'd bite me back.

MRS. FRAAK (*She puts her hand out*) Bite *me*. I want to see if I'm alive.

ANDY Mistress, you mustn't ask me to do that! A dog's nature—a dog's ardor is as close to the surface as those blood-filled veins pulsing in your hand. I might go too far.

MRS. FRAAK Do it. It's an order! Go too far, break the skin, woof it up!

ANDY (*Biting his own paws; he yowls*) Yowl, yowl. Woof, woof, ow.

MRS. FRAAK Are you rabid?

ANDY I don't belong to any faith.

MRS. FRAAK Let me see that paw. Give it to me. (*She examines his paw*) Why did you do it?

ANDY I wanted to see if it really hurt, just in case.

MRS. FRAAK (*Happily*) Just in case you bit me?

ANDY Why ask me to do something I don't *want* to do?

MRS. FRAAK (*She holds his head, opens his mouth, and forces her hand in*) Imagine I'm your worst enemy. (ANDY *hides under the bed*) You're making a fool out of me. Come out. Come out or I'll tell Dr. Fraak you tried to rape me.
(ANDY *crawls out*)

ANDY Okay, I'll bite you, but just a little bite.
(MRS. FRAAK *gives him her hand again and* ANDY *bites it. She gives a tiny cry. He bites again. She cries again, but the microphone is accidentally turned up and a third bite is heard as a scream of terror.* DR. FRAAK *rushes out of the bathroom.* DR. FRAAK *drags* ANDY *into another room.* MRS. FRAAK *nurses her hand.* DR. FRAAK *returns in a fury*)

DR. FRAAK The minute I leave the room you and that dog are at it. I've always hated animals. Especially talking dogs. The least you could have done was give it a dog's name. I resent it! And I'm damn mad. Are you listening to how mad I am?

MRS. FRAAK I'm alive. I'm really alive. Where's the merthiolate? (DR. FRAAK *gets merthiolate from the bathroom and treats her little bite*) I'm excited. I'm really excited.

DR. FRAAK   Punctures infect more easily. I prefer abrasions. There, I've squeezed some bad blood out. Try to control yourself; you've been excited before.

MRS. FRAAK   What a marvelous memory you have! But mine isn't so good. I've forgotten where you go and what you do all night long when you aren't at home.

DR. FRAAK   I never repeat what I never said once. Besides, I don't like to disturb you when you're sleeping.

MRS. FRAAK   I don't know anything about you any more!

DR. FRAAK   What do you want to know?

MRS. FRAAK   I want to know why you spend more time on the upper half of your body than you do on the lower half of mine.

DR. FRAAK   I didn't know you wanted a shave.

MRS. FRAAK   Let's put it this way—

DR. FRAAK   Whatdya want me to do, sprout out of every pore like Andy?

MRS. FRAAK   He's a false issue. I'm sure that if you were as hairy as he is you'd still behave as *you* are, only *you'd* start a flea circus.

DR. FRAAK   Let's put it this way. The ways of man are mysterious.

MRS. FRAAK   Okay, protect me from the knowledge that you are doing nasty things with strangers instead of doing them with me.

DR. FRAAK   You've touched me to the quick. I suppose it's best to tell you everything. The truth is I am a pimp, a pusher, and a cashier, in spite of my ordinary appearance. Every night in the evening I go to an empty building near the waterfront where I keep a sublevel office. This office is my operating room, where

I cut, measure, and weigh what has been delivered. I have three male assistants and one female friend who not only sleeps with me but who goes out and makes pick-ups for me. She is waiting for me now with a large shipment of Mary Jane's from Mexico. That's not all, I'm also an obstetrician and a telephone operator. Need some dimes and nickels?

(*He empties his pockets of about a hundred dimes and nickels.* MRS. FRAAK *pounds on his chest*)

MRS. FRAAK   I hate you!

DR. FRAAK   Keep banging, you'll get your dime back. Are you sure you put one in? (*He throws a handful of coins at her*) Oops, you were right. You've hit the Fraak Pot.

MRS. FRAAK   Don't you ever fight back?

DR. FRAAK   Why should I hit you, my dear, when a pun punishes as well?

MRS. FRAAK (*She reaches under a pillow and brings forth a bitten-into sandwich*)   This is what I did last night: I ate. I ate and I ate and I ate—like this!
(*She bites voraciously into the sandwich. She chews with her mouth open*)

DR. FRAAK   Don't talk while you chew. It isn't exciting to a man.

MRS. FRAAK   If I stop chewing will you stay?

DR. FRAAK   No.

MRS. FRAAK   Don't you think I have a pretty face?

DR. FRAAK   It's a reasonable face.
(*Bored,* DR. FRAAK *gets up to leave*)

MRS. FRAAK   What do you mean, reasonable? And don't be in such a rush.

DR. FRAAK (*Examining her face*) It's a face that won't grow a third eye for spite.
 (ANDY *starts whimpering in the next room*)

MRS. FRAAK Let him out.

DR. FRAAK Not till I go! And from now on shut that mutt up when I'm around or I'll make mush out of his meal.

MRS. FRAAK (*Calling to* ANDY *on the microphone*) In a few minutes, Andy! That's a good dog.

DR. FRAAK (*Muttering*) I know about him. I know about a dog's animal nature.

MRS. FRAAK It's a dog's life he leads, but you have to admit it's an Andy that leads the blind.

DR. FRAAK The blind should stay at home.

MRS. FRAAK That's mean.

DR. FRAAK Mean, is it? Where do you think a dog goes? He goes where he wants to go: a tree, a water hydrant, another dog's ass. That's where a dog wants to take a human being. Degradation needs company. I'm proud to be a man! Proud to hold my nose high where the sweet breezes blow.

MRS. FRAAK Go on. Why stop now? You sounded so noble, standing there on your own *two* legs instead of *down* on all *fours*.

DR. FRAAK You don't care what I talk about or whether I address it to the wall, just so long as I put in some time. Go on, talk, talk!
 (*Mimicking her*)

MRS. FRAAK You are a talented speaker. You do have a verbal pugnacity and wit. The way you said: "I'm proud to be a man!" Why, I almost believed it. I almost forgot that my eggs are active and your sperm is passive! That you refuse to be tested!

DR. FRAAK   I can see you want me to talk. But, Mrs. Toloon-Fraak, I choose my own subjects. You want a lecture, you'll get a lecture; but first—bring me five scallions, two onions, a bud of garlic, soy bean sauce, and some gorgonzola. Also a paring knife, a dinner plate, and don't forget the napkin.

MRS. FRAAK *(Nervously)*   I'll see what I have left.

DR. FRAAK   Improvise, improvise, just don't come back empty-handed; this is to be a demonstration lecture.
> (MRS. FRAAK *goes out.* DR. FRAAK *tests his microphone while she's out, from very loud to soft. There are many sound effects:* galloping horses, water pouring out of a bottle, a frog, hissing steam, *and a* song. MRS. FRAAK *returns with the food and puts it on a small night table.* DR. FRAAK *places the table in front of him like a podium)*

DR. FRAAK   You forgot the salt.

MRS. FRAAK   I salted it already.

DR. FRAAK *(Biting into a scallion)*   So you did. Now watch me very closely. (MRS. FRAAK *watches him very closely as he slowly relishes eating the scallions, onions, etc. She waits until he is done)* Now then. You have just seen me store enough ammunition to launch my secret and dangerous halitotic attack. An art in which breathing is nearly all. Simply stated, my art is to cultivate an evil breath which under certain circumstances—for instance, it will not work in a windstorm—I can direct at a human with drastic results. I had first to create the breath. This took two years of experimenting with various foods and herbs. During this time I tested my weapon against stray dogs and cats. Only when I was able to make them faint from ten feet in the open air, did I feel competent to tackle human beings. You cannot know much of olfaction, so let me be technical for just a moment.

MRS. FRAAK   For two years you experimented! How scientific. How terrific. There's nothing I respect more on earth than the scientific method. First comes the supposition, then the attempt to prove the supposition, step by step, supposing all the way.

DR. FRAAK   I see you've been going through my notes. From now on I'll commit them to memory. However, I want to warn you that whenever I bring my evil breath into play, the odor is worse than a garbage dump, rendering plant, or tannery. The onslaught of its stink is like a physical strike! Beware!

MRS. FRAAK (*Frightened*)   Be where?

DR. FRAAK (*He starts coming at her from behind the table*)   Beware (*He gets to her and then paces ten feet away from her*) One, two, three, four, five, six, seven, eight, nine, ten! First a test at minimal, directed toward an inanimate object, the microphone you are wearing around your neck. Speak into it for the last time tonight!

MRS. FRAAK   Dear husband, I am tired and want to go to sleep. I would beware if I could, but you are set on destroying me. Good luck.

DR. FRAAK   What do you mean by wishing me luck! I'm about to . . . to . . . experiment with you as if you were a stray dog or cat. You couldn't mean less to me. I welcome you with bated breath; I welcome you from my battle station! Prepare!

MRS. FRAAK   Prepare *and* beware? (DR. FRAAK *inhales deeply as if drinking long draughts of cold water. Then he blows out with great strength. The sound effect can be of winds of gale force on the tape.* MRS. FRAAK *speaks into the microphone but it is dead*) Toloon, Toloon, you've done it. I didn't believe you would do it. (*Snapping her fingers into the microphone*) Testing, testing! I'm testing. It's gone. Dead.

DR. FRAAK   I told you I would do it. That was the inanimate triumph! Now for the animate summing up, the crowning glory of my career.

MRS. FRAAK   If you breathe in this direction you'll be disappointed. (*Reaching under the pillow, she takes out a pair of nose plugs*) I've been wearing these every night for two years, to protect myself from you.

DR. FRAAK   Frustrating! I'm left with a "mike" that needs open heart surgery, and a wife who's learned how to handle my secret weapon.

MRS. FRAAK (*She takes the microphone off her neck and hands it to* DR. FRAAK)   The first casualty. I give it to you. While I had it, it gave me electronic communication and distance. Now that is over. I must try to speak low and be heard up close.
   (DR. FRAAK *puts the microphone into his pocket*)

DR. FRAAK   My dear— (*He kisses her breasts*) my own—but not my only one— (*He jumps up*) some day I'm going to start something I can't finish, and then you'll be proud of me.
   (*He exits.* MRS. FRAAK *puts the knife, salt, etc. into the plate and picks it up. She exits*)

MRS. FRAAK (*Her voice is heard offstage*)
   Handy Andy,
   Nice and Dandy,
   Momma's coming
   Ripe and randy.
   (*She whistles for* ANDY)

Blackout

DR. FRAAK's *office, a combination psychiatrist-obstetrical setup. On the desk is a plaster helmet of the human brain. In a bottle on the desk is a large jar of water containing a human fetus, or a rubber doll. Also in the room is an examination table with stirrups, and a leather couch. There are also other chairs. When the scene opens,* DR. FRAAK *is on the couch with* IBOLYA.

IBOLYA Do you love me?

DR. FRAAK You are precious to me. With you I can be young again.

IBOLYA But what can *I* be with you? You ask everybody else all kinds of questions about their childhood, but you don't want to know about mine. It isn't fair. I deserve to be analyzed. I want to talk. I want to be played back on the tape recorder. I want to remember what I used to remember.
(DR. FRAAK *gets up from the couch, puts on his plaster brain, and paces back and forth nervously. He sits down on the edge of the couch and lights a cigarette. He removes the brain helmet and places it like a bowl on the floor. He uses it as an ashtray*)

DR. FRAAK But we are effective without all that. You love and hate me, isn't that enough? I act as your father, your lover, and your employer. I pay in cash, see that you're warm, and receive messages for you on the telephone. I don't lie to you—but I lie to others for you. I buy you books, recommend movies, select your clothes. And I don't sell you cheap! If you're dissatisfied with the percentage you're getting, I'm willing to raise it. You are precious to me—you vile thing.
(*He kisses her. His foot overturns the brain ashtray. He picks it up and puts it back on the desk*)

IBOLYA Is this couch real leather? It smells like it.

DR. FRAAK If you can smell it, it's the real thing.

IBOLYA Well, you do have good taste, but you can afford it! There's lots of things I want, but I can't get 'em.

DR. FRAAK Save up.

IBOLYA Sure! I just saw a pair of knee-high leather boots without seams that lace up the back, and you know what they cost?

DR. FRAAK An arm and a leg?

IBOLYA (*She sidles up to* DR. FRAAK *and puts her hands into the pockets of his lab coat*) Fifty dollars plus tax. Know how many bags that is? Well, I was really up tight when I saw those boots and I'm still sick about not having them. Come on, be a sport.

DR. FRAAK I'd rather listen to you tell me about your childhood than fork over another fifty dollars. My hour is worth twenty-five dollars; that gives me a saving of twenty-five.
  (IBOLYA *pulls away from* DR. FRAAK *and fiddles with things on his desk. She picks up the glass jar with the fetus swimming in it. She peers into it and shakes it up like a malt*)

IBOLYA You couldn't save this! Look, it's moving. It's alive. It wants to come out.

DR. FRAAK Don't drop that! It's a prime example.

IBOLYA (*She puts the bottle back on the desk*) Sure, the fat is whiter and the meat is tender. Get 'em while they're young. (*She puts her arms around* DR. FRAAK) You got me, babe. Come on— let me have the money—don't you know that appearance is everything and style is a way of living.

DR. FRAAK Where'd you read that? Don't tell me.

IBOLYA You always make me beg you. Do you like me to beg? Do you want me to crawl around your office picking up splinters so that you can pry them out with a needle? Oh, Toloon, say you'll be a generous daddy, or I'll be very mad. I might do something terrible like picket your office without any clothes on. Please, you know in front that you're gonna say yes. Make me happy.

DR. FRAAK Tomorrow I'll make you happy, if a certain shipment arrives as planned, but today you'll have to choose another mood.

IBOLYA You know something—you're a real head fucker.

DR. FRAAK You mean a sadist.

IBOLYA Wouldn't you just love to have a label. But you're not enough of what you are to deserve one. I wouldn't be surprised if you turned out to be just a nice guy: an ordinary nice John with a stingy streak; the kind I hate!

DR. FRAAK What kind do you hate?

IBOLYA Creeps! I hate creeps. Say you don't want me now. Why am I here when I could be out shopping? I need make-up, and my hair needs restyling: even you don't like the color it is. Do you have to torture me? Come on. (DR. FRAAK *grabs both her arms very hard. She pulls away*) Make it or don't make it, but let me get the hell out of here.

DR. FRAAK When you're not high you're a stupid, vicious little bitch. And don't pretend you're interested in culture just because your boy friends read you "Kubla-Khan" when they're not on the nod!

IBOLYA I love poetry. I write poetry. Ask me to show you my poems some day.

DR. FRAAK Give me one line of poetry, just one line, and I'll believe you.

IBOLYA "The birds, the flowers, and the sun don't smile any more."

DR. FRAAK Have they ever?

IBOLYA That's the line. Can't you recognize poetry when you hear it?

DR. FRAAK I thought you were kidding.

IBOLYA Just listen to it! "The birds, the flowers, and the sun don't smile any more."

DR. FRAAK Who have they stopped smiling at?

IBOLYA At me. Even innocent children in the street don't smile at me. I'm a dark cloud that makes everything unhappy. Everything I touch turns to shit. I'm so sad. Oh Toloon, I'm so sad.

DR. FRAAK Get on top of it, dear. What you need are some ups. You'll get used to it in time. You'll be able to say to yourself: "Ibolya, it's not you, it's a chemical change."

IBOLYA What's not me?

DR. FRAAK The downs. They're out of your control.

IBOLYA Not really—anyway, it's to your advantage.

DR. FRAAK How? How do you figure that?

IBOLYA If I wasn't depressed I couldn't stand you for two seconds! You're not my type!

DR. FRAAK I'm not my type either. I don't relish the picture I present, but so what?

IBOLYA You're old—

DR. FRAAK Yes—

IBOLYA You're fat—

DR. FRAAK Yes—

IBOLYA And you're not really with it. You're . . . you're ersatz!

DR. FRAAK That's my word, and you're using it against me. What do you think you'll be like when you're forty? You're nothing now; all you have is youth and a flair for imitation of life.

IBOLYA I'll never be forty!

DR. FRAAK Stay as sweet as you are, baby, and pretty soon you won't have a friend in the world. You'll be young and alone in an old room in an old world eating the crumbling plaster from an old wall like a starving infant!

IBOLYA I have friends now. I'll always have friends.

DR. FRAAK Oh yeah? Who are they? Where are they?

IBOLYA They're around. You'll meet them.

DR. FRAAK I'd be delighted to meet your—friends. What do they do?

IBOLYA They're on to a lot of beautiful things.

DR. FRAAK You mean they do nothing? Is that what you mean?

IBOLYA Shut up, you repulsive mother! Don't knock what you don't know.

DR. FRAAK Okay, inform me. Give me the facts. Do they have names? Do they have faces—bodies—occupations? Are they male or female? A subtle blending of both? Do you treat them to my hard-earned cash? Do you amuse them with stories about my corpulent, graceless sex? Are they your contemporaries?

IBOLYA They sing at the Pot Luck, they're more male than you are, and they're called The Feds. They're very famous, and only you wouldn't have heard of them! They're the most beautiful people I know; they're geniuses.

DR. FRAAK   Geniuses—uhuh—but it's old-fashioned to be a genius. There are no geniuses any more—there's facility and publicity—there's volume in sound and volume in sales—no, no geniuses, only promotion.

IBOLYA   How can you analyze anyone if you're so bitter? Just because you're not a genius doesn't mean someone else can't be. You make me puke!

DR. FRAAK   (*He embraces* IBOLYA *and strokes her hair*)   I'm sorry I made you puke. You don't make me puke. You make me feel as if I could eat anything and keep it down.

IBOLYA   Make love to me—I have nothing else to do. I don't have any money to shop with, and it's too early to go out.

DR. FRAAK   I've received more enthusiastic invitations in the past. But that is past—that is all past, and you are the present. You are the here and now—cool—detached—a jet of air absorbing human odors, coiling itself around human desire! You can be weighed, but you're not there. You can soothe me, but when I try to hold you, you rise on my heat. Oh Ibolya, what price pulchritude?
(*He turns his back on her*)

IBOLYA   (*In a shrill, mocking voice*)   Same price as usual.

DR. FRAAK   (*Playing the customer, he feels her up*)   I'm not a stranger. Don't I get a discount?

IBOLYA   The discount is already included; it's automatic.

DR. FRAAK   I'm against automation. Half the fun is in the bargaining. It excites me. It makes me think I really want what I'm bargaining for. Let me have it for less.

IBOLYA   Cheap! Cheat! You knock it down every time I'm with you. Soon you'll be getting it for nothing. And you know what you get for nothing? Nothing!

DR. FRAAK   You're forgetting who I am. What I give you is price-less. I'm your supply depot, your armed guard, your ticket for a trip through inner space. I'm Dr. Toloon-Fraak, who rescued you from your father and is still keeping him at bay; I'm not just any hard-up bastard who walks in off the street!

IBOLYA   Okay, okay, don't rub it in. How much bread *do* you want to lay on me?

DR. FRAAK   Not so fast. We want to do this right. Sex should have an air of mystery, or it will have the stink of familiarity.

IBOLYA   (*Singing out in derision*)   It's fun and games time!

DR. FRAAK   But mystery must have a method. You go over there to my chair and put it on the desk.

IBOLYA   (*She pretends she can't do it*)   Chair's too heavy.

DR. FRAAK   Don't balk—you're a strong and healthy girl.

IBOLYA   (*She shrugs and puts the chair easily on the desk*)   It's up. Now what? Do you want me to scrub the floor in my undies or something?

DR. FRAAK   Sit in the chair. Go on, it's solid, it won't tip. Sit in the chair!
    (IBOLYA *sits in the chair and hoists her skirt above her knees. She leans forward, leering*)

IBOLYA   Can I tell you the story of my life now? It'll be very mys-terious. You'll love the story of my life; it's very touching. I don't know where to begin, but once I received a soul kiss and a belch at the same time, from a friend of my father's who had just finished eating a salami sandwich with pickle in Stanley's Cafeteria. He took me to a "transients or permanent hotel" off of Riverside Drive and tore my new sun-beige nylons trying to get them off without detaching my garters. He didn't pay me and threatened to report me to my father if I made a fuss. Same as you, Dr. Fraak!

DR. FRAAK (*Serious and mad*)   Now sit down and shut up! And try to look sexy! (*Softening, he directs her sweetly*) You are in your workshop window waiting for customers. I walk by and stop. (*He walks by and stops*) You smile. (IBOLYA *smiles*) You hold up ten fingers signifying ten dollars. (IBOLYA *holds up ten fingers*) I hold up five fingers signifying a sharp reduction of fee. (DR. FRAAK *holds up five fingers*) You hold up eight fingers. (IBOLYA *holds up eight fingers*) I counter with seven fingers. (DR. FRAAK *holds up seven fingers*) You smile and invite me in. (IBOLYA *smiles and invites him in.* DR. FRAAK *climbs on the (desk and throws the chair down. He and* IBOLYA *stand up embracing. They begin to make love and sink down on the desk*)

IBOLYA   Your desk is hardly big enough unless I put my feet in the drawers.

DR. FRAAK   I love you, I do—but from now on let me do the talking—let me whisper sweet nothings into your ear.

Curtain

DR. FRAAK's *office.* DR. FRAAK *is walking back and forth thinking when the scene opens.* PSCHUG *rushes in.* DR. FRAAK *staggers back against his desk in surprise.*

PSCHUG   At last I find you, Dr. Toloon-Fraak. Aha, you are right to fall against desk. Is better than to fall on me, Doctor. You fall, I fall, we fall. And for why? For the complete reason you want to knock me down in my life. For the reason I am on your floor too long. Is right? And that big matter of daughter! You have no daughter, is right? I have her here in heart! (*He pounds his chest*) I have her here in head! (*He pounds his head*) But you have her somewhere not moral, impair her health. I want kill you. Maybe then your secret orders pour into the news and she is released. (*He leaps on* DR. FRAAK *and they scuffle*) I am choking you, call the reporters. Take photograph. I am color printer and will develop prints myself for true story.

(DR. FRAAK *pulls away*)

DR. FRAAK   Stop! I can identify you. You won't get away.

PSCHUG   I not run away. I am here for clear the jungle. I have knife. I have net. (*He takes a knife and a small hairnet out of his paper shopping bag*) I have bird whistle. (*He takes an Audubon bird call out of the bag*) I have lion roar.(*He roars*) Your ward N3 in Greenvue Hospital teach me to survive. Your nurse in knowledge with all medical terms, give me eye to eye. She confess her love. But I get idea. I get idea flashing in my head. It flash so bright it blind nurse who is eye to eye with me. It throw her down on bed number four on window side. I say to her: "If you love me, if have love to me, explain in fast terms the location of my daughter Ibolya who is capture with white slavers in the pay of crime king Dr. Toloon-Fraak." Don't get out of my grasp, Doctor. I know I have you now. If you are the crime king, and

I say you are, where you hide your crown? Maybe you give it to Ibolya as sex encouragement pay in advance!

DR. FRAAK Your daughter is in safe hands. She is being taken care of.

PSCHUG She is being taken care of in sin hands. She is being held by swollen fingers with dirty nails and old crust.

DR. FRAAK My diagnosis was correct, Pschug: with you my life is truly in danger.

PSCHUG No danger, Doc. No danger. I little bit crazy but I talk better to deaf ears when I talk loud. (*Shouting*) Hear me, Doc! Where my short kid, Doc? Maybe you bring her to me in church if I wait?

DR. FRAAK Impossible. My wife is like a mother to her. I am like a father to her.

PSCHUG You are not A-1 color printer. You are not like father.
(DR. FRAAK *edges over to* PSCHUG *and as he speaks coaxes him gently to the couch and sits him down*)

DR. FRAAK I seldom take such a personal interest in my patients, Pschug, but the first time I saw you something in your passionate delivery grabbed me and I said to myself: "Dr. Toloon-Fraak, now is the time for you to break out of the mold. Now is the time to experiment. Stop scribbling notes, stop cutting and sewing, stop listening, stop prescribing, stop sitting, stop standing: action is what's needed!" I said to myself: "Here stands Pschug—a run-of-the-mill paranoid-schizo with a very beautiful innocent daughter. What will she do after I put him away? Is it fair to make her a ward of the court when I and my wife could foster her well-being so much better?"
(PSCHUG *stands up*)

PSCHUG Give her to me. I have apartment.

DR. FRAAK No good.

PSCHUG I have job.

DR. FRAAK No good.

PSCHUG I have friend.

DR. FRAAK Who is your friend? Have you told anyone else about this?

PSCHUG My friend is name of Andy. One time I give him dark glasses for Holy Days and he give me his paw in friendship.

DR. FRAAK But Andy is my dog.

PSCHUG Andy is my brother. He tell me all the thing what is bad and I know how it is with Ibolya and we are still to remember who associate with her three times a week and teach smoking and etc.
> (DR. FRAAK *reaches into a desk drawer and takes out a pack of cigarettes*)

DR. FRAAK Here—have a cigarette.

PSCHUG Not one. Give me all. Maybe I teach smoking too. I have lesson to give.

DR. FRAAK (*He throws the whole pack to* PSCHUG) Be my guest.

PSCHUG You are good to guest. Give me food for thought. (*He studies the package*) I think this . . .
> (*He crushes the package in one hand and throws it down as if one second longer in his hand would contaminate him*)

DR. FRAAK Now what good did that do? You can't destroy all the cigarettes in the world. That would be tobaccocide.

PSCHUG And if I crush you, Dr. Fraak? If I crush *you* and you are only *one* Dr. Fraak? What do you call that?

DR. FRAAK   Right now, wishful thinking, a delusion based on the desire for revenge and the misapprehension that you are physically stronger than I am. But let's say, for the sake of non-argument, that you do succeed in killing me—*that*, Pschug, is called murder. A foul way to even up the score.

PSCHUG   But you say I am crazy. If I kill you I deny that these are my hands. "No, not my hands!" I'll swear, "Not my hands! My hands are mainly ignorant of Dr. Fraak. *I* have some cause, they have not."

DR. FRAAK   Fair is foul, and foul is fair; but this is my office, Pschug. People know me in this building, people have seen you come in. Do not abuse me. It is dangerous for you to think you can make up for lost time. Move toward me, and I press this little button under my desk. I'm on my toes with nuts like you, I won't hesitate to summon help. Bear with me, and save your skin. Thou shalt not kill is a sound commandment. You say your daughter is with me? I say she is not. I say she is just passing through. Using Mrs. Fraak and myself as a temporary shelter. Take your time. What is rightfully yours will come back to you. But you cannot chase it and expect it to stand still. If you stop, you may be surprised to find that Ibolya has been looking for you.

PSCHUG   Maybe if I take time, you take Ibolya. You are wicked—

DR. FRAAK (*Reciting*)
    "For every evil under the sun
    There is a remedy or there is none.
    If there be one, seek till you find it;
    If there be none, never mind it."
    Compliments of Mother Goose; you'd better believe it.

PSCHUG   Mother Goose not have in gang position dirty immoral life. She not know this terror case. What she care if I have lost a runaway daughter!

DR. FRAAK   Tell you what I'm gonna do, Pschug. Obviously your breaking point is imminent—so, I'll give you this address— (*He *scribbles the address*) and if you come to the backyard of my house at, say, just before it gets dark tomorrow night—say, about 6:30—Ibolya will come to the window. What happens then is up to you. Don't shout, don't cry, don't jump up and down, that'll frighten her. Just smile and look pleased. She may come running down to you two steps at a time and fall into your arms.

PSCHUG   I will catch her.

DR. FRAAK   (*Pushing* PSCHUG *toward the door*)   Till tomorrow, then.

PSCHUG   If you make me foolish, then I allow myself anything!

Curtain

SCENE 5

The next evening. The bedroom of the Toloon-Fraak's. DR. FRAAK *has been questioning* ANDY.

ANDY   Yes, I know him. His woof appealed to me. Why shouldn't I have accepted his "shades"? The sun was too strong.

DR. FRAAK   It implicates you directly. You should not have taken the gift. Now he expects you to lead him to my little setup and his crummed-up kid. If he gets her, I'm finished!

ANDY   Where is he now?

DR. FRAAK   In the backyard waiting. I had to promise him that he'd be able to see his daughter's face at the window, that she would wave to him and throw him a note.

ANDY   What if he goes to the police?

DR. FRAAK   He's a nut and a crank, they might not take him up on it. But if they do I'll show them my diploma and my calling card that identifies me as a bona-fide professional psychiatrist who is fully able and ready to judge the extent and seriousness of the mental illnessess of the mentally ill.

ANDY   Credentials certainly help when you're up tight!

DR. FRAAK   Yes, and I'd like to sign the old bastard right back in.

ANDY   Woof, woof, master! But what do we do now?

DR. FRAAK   Where's Mrs. Fraak?

ANDY   I left her in bed. We were romping.

34

DR. FRAAK   Get her to glue her face to the window and tell her to wave. Meanwhile I'll write a note to Pschug.

(DR. FRAAK *takes a pad and pencil out of his pocket and, leaning on the wall, writes the note.* ANDY *returns*)

ANDY   She's washing her face to make it look younger and combing her hair to make it longer. From a distance she'll look just like Ibolya. Read me the note.

DR. FRAAK (*He reads*)   Dear Dad . . . How I wish I could be with you now, but I am just getting over a cold and can't. Perhaps we can meet next week and talk. I am a good girl and a loving daughter. Wipe all bad thoughts from your mind. It's all in your mind. Look up and see how happy and clean I am. Soon we will be together, I am sure, but not now. If you leave your address and phone number with the doorman I'll get in touch with you. You can trust the doorman, he delivers messages for everyone in the house. I remain your devoted daughter who never forgets you . . . Ibolya.

ANDY   It's practically a letter. Can I fold it? I need practice with my paws. There are so many things a man can do with his hands that a dog only dreams of.

(DR. FRAAK *hands the paper to* ANDY, *who flattens and smoothes it on the floor. Then he folds it*)

DR. FRAAK   What did you say to Mrs. Fraak? What did you tell her to get her to follow my orders? She must know nothing of this. I don't like to worry her. I don't like to involve her in my private practice.

ANDY   I told her that a beggar was begging, a beggar whose dog I used to be, and that once I had promised this beggar a glimpse of a lovely lady if he let me go; and that now he had come to collect. That he was downstairs in the backyard waiting to feast his bleary, sticky, mean eyes on her and that if she didn't smile and wave and press her face against the pane like a child he'd take me away with him and she'd never be able to romp with me again.

35

DR. FRAAK You understand Mrs. Fraak well, Andy; she's just a princess at heart.

ANDY I wouldn't roll over and play dead for any other mistress.

DR. FRAAK But what would you do for your master? Eh, Andy, what would you do for me?

ANDY I'd jump through a hoop for you.

DR. FRAAK Andy, you're a prince of a dog.

Blackout

SCENE 6

DR. FRAAK *is seated in his office with his back to the audience. The office is brightly lit. He turns around with his chair to face the audience.*

DR. FRAAK (*To the audience*)   The thing I rely on is the good will of my patients, not my *former* patients. Pschug is a former patient and he has forgotten what we both discovered together: that the line of least existence is preferable to going out of your way. He wants to destroy my reputation, but let him beware, I have none.

Blackout

*There are sounds of soft, unnerving laughter. The lights go up
on an empty stage.* PSCHUG *appears carrying a plant. He sits down
on the stage and removes his shoes. He spits on his feet and polishes
them with a dirty handkerchief. He blows his nose into the handkerchief. He twirls the handkerchief into a ribbon and ties it
around his head. He clears his throat a few times and peers out at
the audience.*

PSCHUG   I will find you, but nobody will be there, bad girl!
     (PSCHUG *shrugs his shoulders, turns back to the audience
     and pees into his plant. He picks up the plant and leaves the
     stage)*

Blackout

DR. FRAAK's *office.* THE FEDS *are singing and playing guitars.* DR. FRAAK *is helping* IBOLYA *onto the examination table.*

THE FEDS (*Singing*)
> You're not in my bag, baby,
> I write my own tag, baby,
> Go screw on a mountain,
> Your youth ain't my fountain,
> You're not in my bag, baby.
> In fact you're a drag, baby,
> Go screw in a lay-ay-ache,
> Or cry at my way-ay-ache,
> That's what you get for wantin' me,
> That's what you get for wantin' me.

DR. FRAAK (*To* IBOLYA) Please remove your clothing. (IBOLYA *pulls her dress off*) Your slip too. Can't operate with our hands tied, can we? (IBOLYA *removes her slip and sits on the edge of the examining table in her brassiere and panties. She is huge in front and has a stuffed pillow taped to her*) Open your mouth and say "ah."
> (DR. FRAAK *kisses her on the neck*)

IBOLYA Ah. AAAHHH!
> (DR. FRAAK *listens to her heart with his stethoscope*)

DR. FRAAK I hear it. Good strong beat, Ibolya. (*He does a tap dance in rhythm to her heart. The sound of her heartbeat is heard over a loudspeaker on tape. Her heart goes faster and faster till* DR. FRAAK *falls to the floor. He rises with dignity and resumes the examination*) I used to be pretty good, never missed a beat. Never missed a step. Guess I can't keep up any more. (*He applies his stethescope to the pillow*) I know it's in there, but I can't hear it. This calls for immediate surgery. (*To* THE FEDS) Boys, I'll need your help. This is going to be a difficult delivery.

THE FEDS (*Singing*)
Need some light, Doc?
Is it right, Doc,
That no tic-toc can be heard?
In the night, Doc,
What a sight, Doc,
Fix the tic-toc for my bird.
> (DR. FRAAK *cuts the pillow open with a large wire cutter or metal shears. When he has cut it open sufficiently he rolls his sleeves up and digs in*)

DR. FRAAK If my wife ever caught me with my hands in the belly of someone else's pillow, she'd slice off my hands. She can do as much with her lady-size dainty as I can do with my old fashioned.

IBOLYA Is it going to be all right, Doc?

DR. FRAAK (*He pulls a fistful of pot out of the pillow and examines it*) Outside of an excess of twigs, I'd say it was good quality, very good quality.

IBOLYA Thank God.
> (IBOLYA *moans and writhes*)

DR. FRAAK Easy now, mother, it must have a big head on it. Takes after you. We'll have you emptied in a minute. Boys, my instruments. (THE FEDS *bring strainers, bags, a small scale, wax paper, tin foil, and cigarette rolling paper.* DR. FRAAK *and* THE FEDS *go about their work, straining and measuring and weighing and rolling till the pillow is emptied.* IBOLYA *sits up*) Congratulations, you are now the mother of a pleasant pastime. Take her to the recovery room, boys, and remove the tape. She deserves a maternity treat, a chance to watch her child for the first time. A chance to dream of its future accomplishments while holding it.
> (THE FEDS *exit singing, leaving* DR. FRAAK *to vacuum, with*

a miniature vacuum cleaner, the tea that has fallen on the floor)

THE FEDS and IBOLYA
It's green, it's green, it's mexiscene.
It's pot, it's pot, it's much a lot.
It's pure, it's pure, get high for sure.
Come on and make it, take the cure.
(*The office blacks out. The next room lights up and can be seen through a transparent scrim.* IBOLYA *is nude. She is swaying and talking to* THE FEDS. THE FEDS *pass a stick around.* IBOLYA *takes a long drag*)

IBOLYA   Mmmmmmm. Pot makes me feel so sexy. Like a pot of pot. (IBOLYA *sings*)
I got the boudoir blues,
Don't have time to take off my shoes.
When the Johns know I'm in town,
Isn't long before they've got me down
On a divan, or a pillow, or a table, or the floor.
And they always are a screamin'—Baby, give me more.

I got the bedroom reds,
It's gettin' so I can't count heads.
If I ask a guy: "Say, what's your name?"
He says: "I told you last night, and it's still the same."

On a corner, in an alley, in an attic like Svengali,
And they always are a screamin'—Baby, give me more.

I don't know what I've got,
But I'm glad that it's a lot.
I don't know where I'll be,
But, it won't be up a tree.
I don't know how to cope
If my bowl don't have no dope.
Sure I don't know who I am,
But I can't ask Uncle Sam.
I don't know how I'll make it.
Life's a handout and I'll shake it.

Yes, I don't know what I've got,
But I sure don't plan to rot
On a divan, or a pillow, or a table, or the floor,
Tho they'll always keep a screamin'—Baby—more, more, more!
(*The telephone rings.* IBOLYA *answers it*)
Hello. Who is it? Some nut is just breathing on the other end. Come on, who is it? Say, call me later and we'll talk some more.
(IBOLYA *is about to hang up when the voice of* PSCHUG *booms out*)

PSCHUG (*Over the phone*)   Where are you? Here I am thinking how to find you on the North Side, thinking I tear you apart into screams and lies. I have prophecy! Though you disappear into apartments, into kidnappers, into disease and private numbers, into bad gums and teeth fall out, into lawyers who ask me three thousand dollars and make it snappy or more guilty mixed hands. I speak! And I will find you to unwash guilty hands with my proof, am I not that person!
(IBOLYA *hangs up shocked*)

IBOLYA   He'll kill me if he finds me. (*The phone rings again.* IBOLYA *picks it up*) You'll never get me. I'll jump out the window.

PSCHUG (*Over the phone*)   I love little baby who when home is virgin and happy, have good moral and religion life.

IBOLYA   I'm a big girl now. Stop bothering me. I don't want to remember you.

PSCHUG (*Over the phone, singing*)
I remember you with your warm bottom,
Your warm bottom, your warm heart,
And the name Ibolya resting in your thighs.
(IBOLYA *slams the receiver down; she dresses in a hurry.* THE FEDS *help her. They put everything into a bag* (*an airlines bag?*), *including the phone, and they go out*)

Blackout

The scene opens in DR. FRAAK's *office. He is dusting off his couch and plumping up a pillow preparatory to taking a nap. He is humming insanely. There is a plaster cast of the human brain on his desk. It is hollow. He puts it on his head like a helmet and strides around.*

DR. FRAAK   My brains will protect me, or . . . (*He takes off his helmet and stares at it*) . . . I'll dash my brains out on the floor. (*The phone rings.* DR. FRAAK *puts the helmet back on the desk and answers the phone*) Yes? Oh yes, sweetheart, I was just about to ring you up. I'm sleeping at the office tonight. Yes, piles and piles of notes, transcriptions, evaluations, conversations, and consequential apathies. I'm not making it up. What am I really doing? Well, really I was thinking of dashing my brains out on the floor. My brain and I are quite alone. I know that you're alone too. Yes, we're both alone, but you have Andy. I know Andy is just a dog. But he *is* a talking dog! He doesn't say the right things? What do you want him to say? What do you want me to say? You want me to be lab tested? What if I don't light up after you've screwed me into the socket? Everything is funny. I'll joke if I want to. What? Someone called you up and accused you of keeping his child? What did you say? Andy told you what to say? He told you to say that Ibolya is in trouble? Who the hell is Ibolya? It sounds fanciful. No, I don't know her! You are *waiting* for the man who spoke to you on the phone? Aren't you frightened? It might be a former patient of mine. Call the police. You won't? You're bored—you want to meet someone as passionate as you are? You're not passionate, you're imagining it. I warn you not to try to find out. Wait, no wait, don't hang up, let me. Let me hang up first. I'm hanging up. U-P spells (*He hangs up the phone slowly and finally*) hanging up. (*He rummages around in his desk and finds some pills. He takes a few dozen with a glass of water and lies down on the couch. He caresses himself*) It's only a matter of time before I sleep. I can handle myself better if I get a little sleep. That's nice, smooth out all the wrinkles. (*He touches his face like a blind person*) I'd know myself anywhere. (*Fingering the folds in his face*) I sun myself in the valleys, and on the same day, if I want to, I can go skiing down the mountains. (*His whole palm slides down his nose*) My body is a resort. A last resort.

 (*He falls asleep*)

Blackout

Act Two

IBOLYA *is alone onstage. She is reading from the* I Ching (The Book of Changes), *or a tape of her reading may be heard instead. She is reading* The Parts of the Body. *As she reads, the proper tri-grams are projected onto the background. Also onstage are a mirror and a small table. A huge mexican paper flower, in very bright oranges and reds is somewhere.*

IBOLYA (*Reading*)   "The parts of the body. The creative manifests itself in the head, the receptive in the belly, the arousing in the foot, the gentle in the thighs, the abysmal in the ear, the clinging in the eye, keeping still in the hand, the joyous in the mouth." (*She then moves—dances or pantomimes—to the words*) "The head governs the entire body. The belly serves for storing up. The foot steps on the ground and moves; the hand holds fast. The thighs under their covering branch downward; the mouth in plain sight opens upward. The ear is hollow outside; the eye is hollow inside."

(*There is a blackout. Then the lights go up suddenly.* IBOLYA *is still standing onstage, either nude or in a body stocking. She remains motionless*)

Blackout

SCENE 2

The bedroom of the TOLOON-FRAAKS. PSCHUG *and* MRS. FRAAK *confront each other.*

MRS. FRAAK   So you are Pschug!

PSCHUG   Father of Ibolya. (*Looking around the room*) Produce her.

MRS. FRAAK   But I can't. I don't have her. I don't even know who she is.

PSCHUG   Your husband who have great combined factors on earth, who organize torment eternal, who have conversation with devil in hell to make Ibolya hate me, for shame me, he tell me you are mother for her.

MRS. FRAAK   I don't believe it!

PSCHUG   I believe it. I must believe it. I have proofs speak to me by the hour. The papers do not publish these thing. I no shame! I have prophecy! Is it reasonable that once God breathed into her nostrils the breath that all diving creature breathe? He gave her animated to the body. He made the lady and the man stood up, and lived! See numbers 31:28. That is why in miracle I am closer to Ibolya. She is here!

MRS. FRAAK   No. I don't believe she even exists. Why don't you call Dr. Fraak's answering service. He's the one you ought to see. He'll tell you who exists and who doesn't.

PSCHUG   I ask you!

MRS. FRAAK   I can't tell you if I don't know. We all have our troubles. Can I bring you a cup of tea?

48

PSCHUG   The whole world saying not think! But I think it's an overtone campaign, but I not resign.

MRS. FRAAK   I'm glad I asked you over. You have strength of character. Come here, I want you closer.

PSCHUG   Ha, ha, lady. Ha, ha, in your stranger face.

MRS. FRAAK   You did manage to have a daughter?

PSCHUG   I say yes. You not believe to me.

MRS. FRAAK   Maybe I do believe to you. I'm beginning to believe you.

PSCHUG   God bless you.

MRS. FRAAK   You have great energy. Great thrust. And you should be relieved of your great anxiety so that you can achieve once again your great energetic thrust. Your daughter is not here, but perhaps I can help you find her.

PSCHUG   Good! We must be fast in her footsteps!

MRS. FRAAK   Not so fast! I can't just rush into this thing without doing some research on it.

PSCHUG   (*He reaches into his bag and starts pulling out his tapes and bundles of letters and rags*)   Stop! Look! And listen!

MRS. FRAAK   No, no, Pschug; we must start at the beginning. I want to know about Ibolya before she was born. How she was conceived. (*Getting sexy*) How you conceived of it.

PSCHUG   Well, we settled in no-man's-land in Grove Street, number 326.

MRS. FRAAK   A young, energetic number.

PSCHUG   In the now heart of Greenwich Village, next door to the coal oil Johnny soap factory where I think they used dead horse fat make soap.

MRS. FRAAK   Yes.

PSCHUG   My wife is bad to be so close to factory, but I not move. She say to me: "Pschug, get out fast, or you will look good in a box with plenty of flowers." As I said: "That is what you think you want—lose me, you be surprise when I die. You will be sorry as all of city have great floating smell." Well, she said she was afraid of Pschug to doctor who turn her lung inside out. She say: "That man is caged lion and as I think he is ready to kill me." I not like to be hate! Is against religion. I was going to pray but— I go out in fog. I am sorry to her. I promise furniture all kinds, repaired, polish, upholstered, mattresses cushion made over and to order drapes and slipcover made to order. No, no! She scream no! I want breath, I want baby, I want clean blood. She went crazy. She say: "Why I can't have this thing? This transfushion. You must respect to me. I done thirteen years in marriage." And it grew on me in earnest that it my fault. All my moneys went out to her. I was tops. We move to new place, no phony stuff clean air and front room.

MRS. FRAAK   Yes?

PSCHUG   I was her regular fan. I like hear her sing fifteen minutes so natural. I like see her make tea so strong with three teaballs. As doctor say: "She poison you with three teaballs." But I talk to him: "Doctor, you are no professor. Strong man, strong tea." I don't think I have her as enemy since I give her all kinds money when she sleep with me even as wife. And what do you think, she was starving?

MRS. FRAAK   But when I offered you a cup of tea you refused.

PSCHUG   I not answer to you because of personal memories.

MRS. FRAAK   I too have personal memories, but they are too numerous to mention and very uninteresting. I've never conceived.

PSCHUG   Unfortunate woman.

MRS. FRAAK   I don't ask for money, just for love.

PSCHUG   Sin not! I pass it on to someone in need like you. Like you
was a friend through my life. I fight with the devil always kidding: man has soul, man has no soul, soul people in the world
are kings and queens. Every word is the truth.
    (MRS. FRAAK, *growing bored, lights a cigarette, inhales, and
    keeps the smoke in her mouth. She bends forward swiftly
    and kisses* PSCHUG *on the mouth, filling his mouth with
    smoke. He, chokes on it and coughs. She bangs him on the
    back*)

MRS. FRAAK   I never inhale, it makes me dizzy. How do you feel?

PSCHUG   I feel, if you ask for money, you get love. Just one minute
I hide my proofs; is not for them to see (PSCHUG *hides his shopping bag under the mattress*) Now I have free time to make new
conception. Where there is smoke there is fire. Ha, ha, I learn
American saying. But I not forget Ibolya. After I have done this
thing with you, we go find my daughter.
    (*They embrace*)

Blackout

SCENE 3

PSCHUG *and* MRS. FRAAK *are in bed, in the bedroom of the* TOLOON-FRAAKS. ANDY *enters with a little black book between his teeth.*

MRS. FRAAK Andy, what have you got? Give it to me.
     (ANDY *trots over to her*)

ANDY I thought it was your address book. I found it in the bathroom.

MRS. FRAAK No, mine is bound in Morocco. This is someone else's.
     (MRS. FRAAK *leafs through the address book silently*) Pschug, I want you to hear this. Pschug, darling! Wake up!

PSCHUG Yes, I wake up. I have new command over English language. Two hour with you, Mrs. Fraak, and I say anything in my best abbreviation. To make it short, hiya kiddo!

MRS. FRAAK This may come as a shock. I have evidence that can cause a huge scandal. Your daughter seems to be involved and so does my husband.

PSCHUG Ibolya, tell me of Ibolya!

MRS. FRAAK This is her book. It has the name of the owner here on the first page. (*She shows it to him*) At first glance, it looks harmless, ordinary, but when the first name on the list happens to be a millionaire, it just isn't the . . . the milieu a girl like your daughter would automatically fall into. I mean, it's suspicious. I'll read the book to you. I'll pick out the kind of names that belong in someone else's book. And what is more, there are prices after the names. (MRS. FRAAK *gets out of bed in her nightgown and stands center stage. She reads the address book as if she were at a poetry reading*) Ron Rake Pastor, Lu 8-4776, $50. Ibolya, ½ Tina. Bailor, Dimitrios, Hotel Salery, Room 11B, Bh 4–2211, same names, same price. Bunny Brimstone, Tx 4–8276, Ibolya, Jean Hervey, $100. Three-legs Bellini, 625 Stark Avenue, Apt. 12C, Ba 8–2222. Ibolya, Nida, $50. plus. Torpedo Smith, Our Savior Gluegut, Fred Loozits, P.H.C. Oh, it goes on and on . . . names; names like Fox Feelman, Brice Fartford, Dork Bruin, Ham Galspy, Timothy Oozejelly, and Mick Hobbleoff.

PSCHUG   Stop the names! What it means?

ANDY   It means your daughter is a poet.

PSCHUG   What it means, Fred Loozits, P.H.C.?

ANDY   I have an idea. Tape P for pot and what've you got? Take H for horse and you're in the saddle. Take C for cocain and you've got it again!
(*He does a shuffle*)

MRS. FRAAK   Just yesterday I read his name in the papers. It was his fiftieth wedding anniversary. Top hat and cane, a smile for everyone. He was one of Dr. Fraak's wealthier private patients.

PSCHUG (*Agitated*)   It sound like masquerade party of gang interest. Attention competent department! White slavery traders, racketeers, kidnapping, immoral terror gang interest. My daughter named and written down. Ibolya $50. Ibolya $100. Ibolya many bucks, what it means?

MRS. FRAAK   My blood runs cold. I'm terrified. (*Over-dramatic*) Poor, poor husband, poor Dr. Fraak: At first he used in private, alone, to perform medical miracles. I couldn't stop him. He wrote his own prescriptions. In the morning he'd ask me to bend his spoon for him and then he'd light his bunsen burner. "Here goes!" he'd say, "the lovin' spoonful."

ANDY   He's the master and he's clean. You misinterpret his experiments. Dr. Toloon-Fraak is a benefactor to mankind. That's the kind of man he is.

MRS. FRAAK Sure.

PSCHUG I am exhaust. Who are these names? What are they doing? I kill them. I invite them to immortal party. I give them to drink. I give them to eat. I give them Ibolya in familiar. And then I give them to think!

MRS. FRAAK It's much too dangerous to take direct action.

PSCHUG Repent! I will say to them, repent! Repent and protect your life. Then I will show them real man. Old man. Crazy old man in his only one world body. In his body of no abuse, no drug, no girl. In his kept body made of the Lord. They take my only and good and beautiful person, my virgin, (*Whispering*) who when home have religion. (*Shouting*) They are big men, but I am great too! Have I not travel in airplane when even Shakespierre did not! When even Colombus did not! And who can be this Ham Galspy?

MRS. FRAAK A movie producer.

PSCHUG Ron Rake Pastor?

MRS. FRAAK I told you, a millionaire.

PSCHUG There are some lost things that money cannot buy! Give me book. I want to give these name to my memory. (*MRS. FRAAK gives him the address book*) Aha! Dimitrios Bailor? A pilot?

MRS. FRAAK A composer and conductor.

PSCHUG Three-legs Bellini?

MRS. FRAAK A designer.

PSCHUG And the one who misrepresent his calling? The one who call himself Our Savior Gluegut!

MRS. FRAAK Our Savior leads a Latin American band.

PSCHUG   Brice Fartford?

MRS. FRAAK   A collector of porcelain pots.

PSCHUG   Here, take back the book, Mrs. Toloon-Fraak. (*She takes it*) So, it come to this. What is in mind? What is in work? Not enough? I was joke when I say I give party. They, all the Mr. Booknames get up in morning—wash face in champagne, dry face on young girl, throw on floor. Not need be careful. Everything expensive. Everything fine. I will fine them and maybe I die in their sight! They never see crazy old man die. They not pay cash for that! They make for talk to me sincere: "Please, Pschug, you no die." Very sincere. Oh yes, they very sincere but not like me! Not sincere to die *without* my heart stop. Oh no, not believe to me that I ring bell, dead, walk in, dead, shake hand, dead, and spit in face dead! I cannot speak no more.

ANDY   I'm glad I'm not human. If I had my choice I'd rather be a machine. Machines mean something to people.

MRS. FRAAK   You're judging from the outside.

ANDY   Aren't we all carnivorous.

MRS. FRAAK   The difference is, Andy, that I use a toothpick and you cannot.

PSCHUG   Come on. We find Dr. Fraak and show him this, this black book!

Blackout

SCENE 4

ANDY *trots onstage. He sniffs around, trots again, and stops to dig for a bone. He barks at shadows, then settles down, stage-front, for a snooze. Thus he exercises his true dog nature.*

Blackout

DR. FRAAK's *office. He is still sleeping.* MRS. FRAAK, ANDY, *and* PSCHUG *tiptoe in.*

PSCHUG Shhhhhh! (*He searches the place for* IBOLYA) I expected nothing.

MRS. FRAAK Andy, you wake the doctor. He loves your bark. He won't get up mad if you wake him.

PSCHUG If a man called Dr. Toloon-Fraak is mad, it not because of wake up.

MRS. FRAAK I never could face his anger, especially when I've said something too cruel.

ANDY Say something too cruel now. I'll protect you.

MRS. FRAAK Stay close to me, Andy, in case he strikes out. Promise you'll bite him this time.

ANDY If the necessity arises, I bite!
(ANDY *growls*)

MRS. FRAAK (*Bending over* DR. FRAAK) Calling Dr. Toloon-Fraak, Dr. Toloon-Fraak. Emergency! Dr. Toloon-Fraak! Calling Dr. Pimp-Fraak. Adultery! Please come to Ward-off! Please come to Ward N3. Adultery! Emergency! Dr. Toloon-Fraak.

DR. FRAAK (*Rising in a trance*) Yes, nurse. I'm on my way. (*He tramps up and down in place*) Well, what is it, nurse? Bed number six acting up? I told you to increase the sedative. If you don't do what I tell you to do. I'll go out of my headitive. That's the best meditive. I've said all I want to saiditive. How about a date tonight? I'll clear some space on the operating table, or would you rather slide down the laundry chute with me? Sure, I'll wait till your laundry's dirty. What do you think I am? I hear you've been eye to eye with my most difficult patient, a Mr. Pschug. I want to apprise you of my medical findings concerning him. He has nits multiplying in his eyelashes. Haven't you noticed?

MRS. FRAAK   I haven't noticed. My eyes were closed. My nose was stuffed. The steam went on in my underpanting. I haven't found him difficult at all, just a trifle clumsy when he kissed my tumsy.

DR. FRAAK   I won't stand for it. I'll have you transferred to the diet kitchen. I'll have you counting salt crystals seven days a week, four weeks a month, twelve months a year. I'll—

MRS. FRAAK   I'm not the only nurse who's done worse.

PSCHUG   Dr. Fraak, I have daughter Ibolya. Here is A-1 color photograph.
      (PSCHUG *gives him a photograph*)

DR. FRAAK (*Examining the photo*)   The warm colors are bleeding into the whites. Hand me the sterile cotton, nurse. (*He dabs the photo*) There she is. I like the way you've had her pose. Modest, virginal, legs crossed, arms at sides, mouth closed, eyes cast down, hair in bun. Perfect, perfect. A real challenge in this nut world of shells that crack themselves open out of season.

PSCHUG   Let me out, Doc. I take care of her welfare.

DR. FRAAK   It'll be a long time, Pschug, a long, long, timerino. Why don't you put on your bathrobe and go down to the game room? Make friends with the other fellows. Challenge them to a game of scripture memory. Or play a game of checkers with yourself and win. Some of my most depressed cases play games with themselves, and it cheers them up when they realize that if they choose their team carefully it makes all the difference.

PSCHUG   Why you keep Ibolya's picture, Doc?

DR. FRAAK   You don't want it stolen, do you? The floor nurse will keep it for you. When you want to see it, just ask her to show it to you. I'll verify the request with my authority. And by the way, don't eat the crayons, a waxy stool doesn't paint a pretty picture!

ANDY   Woof, woof, woof, woof.

DR. FRAAK   Nurse! Get that dog out of here; he's contaminating my ham and cheese. He's clogging the ventilation system. He's dragging sterilized gauze through the hallway.

MRS. FRAAK   Your ward is wild, Doctor. They think there's going to be a party. They want to dress up in costume. They all want to get a prize.

DR. FRAAK   Paint their pills purple and string them up. Why not have a party.

MRS. FRAAK   I think it would be excellent for the patients if we invited some outsiders, Dr. Fraak. Here is your address book. (*She hands him the little black address book*)

DR. FRAAK (*Hypnotically flips through the pages*)   Big people like this won't want to donate their time.

MRS. FRAAK   But doctor, this is Mental Health Week. Mental Health certainly comes before Muscular Dystrophy.

DR. FRAAK   We can try, nurse. We can try. And if they're a trifle hesitant, I know what to offer them—an incentive.

MRS. FRAAK   What do you have in mind, Doctor?

DR. FRAAK   Women—and in extremely reluctant cases—drugs.

MRS. FRAAK   Women?

DR. FRAAK   The wartiest in the ward.

MRS. FRAAK Can you get them to co-operate?

DR. FRAAK They're on the reward system; a few bills and they'll do anything. It's the cash and carry syndrome.

MRS. FRAAK Oh, Toloon—

DR. FRAAK Doctor Fraak!

MRS. FRAAK Oh, Dr. Fraak, do you think we can ask Our Savior Gluegut to bring his Latin American band here?

DR. FRAAK I have his number. I'll call him.

MRS. FRAAK And all the rest in the book, all the rest—call them too! They can take it off their income tax. Oh, I wish that Brice Fartford would decorate our corridors with his marvelous collection.

DR. FRAAK Nurse—nurse, I want you to put Pschug into solitary confinement the night of the party. It might disturb him. He's a recidivist of the worst kind. Also, I want you to send an invitation to Miss Ibolya Pschug, his daughter. I want to know more about the relationship; and I am sure she would like to view the progressive methods used here first hand: how people are treated not only like people, but like people who *like* people, and are ready and able to pay for it. If you need me, I'll be in my office.
  (*He lies down on the couch again*)

MRS. FRAAK Andy, that hospital meant more to him than anything else on earth. He wanted to impress the trustees so that they'd increase his budget and enable him to pour money into his special projects.

ANDY That's why he's so doped up now. The committee refused his request. He mentioned a theater wing he was planning: a psychodrama building with four floors: one floor for the super-ego, another for the egolet, another for the ego on your face, and at the top—the American ego.

MRS. FRAAK   How do you know so much?

ANDY   I know everything but my last name.

PSCHUG (*scrutinizing* DR. FRAAK) Maybe he kill Ibolya not to share her with me. Why does he look wrong?

MRS. FRAAK   We have to wait till his bloodstream is clear, then he'll wake up and talk to us. Although I think he's told us what we want to know.
(PSCHUG *goes off to the side of the stage, looking for* IBOLYA *in cabinets and under the stage and behind the stage. Then, very cautiously,* IBOLYA *and* THE FEDS *sneak in*)

IBOLYA   Hello. If you're waiting for the doc, you'll have a long wait. (*She lifts* DR. FRAAK's *head and lets it drop*) He's out. Whatdya want?

MRS. FRAAK   To see you!

IBOLYA   Take a good look. Here I am.

MRS. FRAAK   You could never be my daughter.

IBOLYA   Don't you care for me? Am I too wide in the lips? Am I too high in the nose? And what's the difference anyway! Why don't you come back during office hours and tell it to the tape?

ANDY   *This* is Mrs. Toloon-Fraak!

IBOLYA   How do you write your name?

ANDY   I said this is MRS. Toloon-Fraak!

IBOLYA   Then she's come to the right place.

ANDY   She's my *mistress* and the *wife* of Dr. Toloon-Fraak!

IBOLYA   Where'd she break her act in—Tijuana?

MRS. FRAAK (*To* IBOLYA) You're a terrible new generation!

IBOLYA Me?

MRS. FRAAK You, yes, you!

ANDY She's not so new—she's been put up for sale before.

IBOLYA (*To the audience*) It's like I don't feel cool any more.
(*Swaying*) I keep wondering—
    (*Singing*)
Where is all the sunshine?
Where is all the sun?
Where has daylight ended?
Where has night begun?

MRS. FRAAK You don't want to know! Have you ever tried to find
out? How do you spend the day? Give me your typical day!

IBOLYA and THE FEDS (*Singing with a guitar. They are spirited,
shooting, falling, tumbling, dancing. They sing the song twice*)
    This is the way we spend the day,
    Wake up late with feet of clay,
    Try to walk,
    Decide to talk,
    Buy a gun,
    And shoot some chalk.
    Rat-a-tat-tat
    That's where we're at!
        (PSCHUG *rushes back very excited.* IBOLYA *hides behind* THE
        FEDS. PSCHUG *has found a bag of bones. He empties them
        on stage. He takes a tape measure out of his shopping bag
        and measures the bones*)

PSCHUG It is she! From knee to ankle it is in proper length. And
this— (*Holding up a bone*) is female round. It is she! And here;
notice the recent meat of finished appetite. Some fiend have
digest her in his loops. Who can be so hungry?

ANDY Those are mine, if you don't mind. That is my stash. Those
are not the bones Ibolya was, those are butcher-bought for me

alone. I am a dog. You won't deny me my bones to slobber over. (ANDY *takes a bone and gnaws at it*) Dirty or clean, I don't like them lean. Give me some meat and watch me eat.

> (*He eats and bounces around the room with the bone. He stops and eats again.* IBOLYA's *voice is heard, but she is still hiding*)

IBOLYA   Promise you won't hit me.
> (*There is a felt, silent pause*)

PSCHUG   Ibolya! Ibolya, where are you? Speak.
> (IBOLYA's *voice again; she is still hiding*)

IBOLYA   Promise you won't take me with you.

PSCHUG   Don't ask me. Appear!
> (*The voice of* IBOLYA *comes from her hiding place*)

IBOLYA   Promise.

PSCHUG (*Straining his gaze, he sees a bit of her dress*)   I see you. Come out. All of you is holy. My hands are hand in hand. They not hit. I want to be sweet. I want my life to live in work and pray for you. Come—

> (IBOLYA *comes out slowly, carefully; she walks toward* PSCHUG. *When he doesn't move she feels more confident and adopts the walk of a slut. An evil grin corrodes her face*)

MRS. FRAAK   Pschug—her face—she hates you! Don't take her back.

> (THE FEDS, *who have been tuning their guitars in a corner, start to sing and play. Before this they have been underlining the action and words of the others with appropriate mock movie music*)

THE FEDS (*Singing*)
> He was too mad, and that is bad,
> He was too loud in any crowd.
> In anger banged her on the head,
> From that time on she wished him dead.

IBOLYA (*Facing* PSCHUG)   I, I'm—

PSCHUG (*With emotion*)   *Ibolya!*

IBOLYA   I, I'm—

PSCHUG   Speak! I listen you. Happy to wash all mixed guilty hands. Happy to hold you. (*He embraces her in a bear hug*) Happy to have justice. I not care my personally documents disappear. I will demand assistance for their search in U.S.A. I make more life savings in joint account. Two names together; either/or Ibolya, Pschug! *Mr.* Pschug!

IBOLYA   I, I'm—broke right now. Could you lend me five dollars till the end of the week? I expect a job then. It's all set. They promised to call me up. Couldya let go of me now!

PSCHUG   I not know how to let go. Speak more. I want hear how you need me. Sure, I crazy old man, but I work hard. Have hard muscle!
(*Pulling her to him in an iron embrace*)

IBOLYA (*She rests her head on his shoulder*)   What do I do now—faint or scream?

PSCHUG   You stay!

IBOLYA   You didn't answer me about the money, because with or without it, I'm getting out of here. I have appointments.

PSCHUG   You stay. Money no object! You stay because I want!

ANDY   Let her go, Pschug; she's rotten to the core. If she wants to kill herself, let her.

PSCHUG   I never hear dog be nasty before. One more word and I kick you—dumb animal!

IBOLYA   Kick him, Dad, kick him in the balls.

PSCHUG (*Sentimentally*) Ibolya, you call me Dad. You call me Dad!

IBOLYA Say, I can hardly breathe. Willya leggo?

PSCHUG What you do if I let go?

IBOLYA I dunno? Why—what's the right answer? Whatever I say, you won't like it.

PSCHUG You hate me; you act like you hate Pschug!

MRS. FRAAK (*To* THE FEDS) Why don't you get her away from him? Cowards!

ONE OF THE FEDS Cool it, man! We dig the family reunion.

MRS. FRAAK Why don't you sing a song?

ONE OF THE FEDS I got a lump in my throat. They got two lumps in their throats. We're about to cry with joy. (THE FEDS *make the guitars cry; then they sing*)
    Yeah, yeah, yeah, yeah, yeah, yeah,
    Yeah, yeah, yeah.
    Never trust a dancing daughter,
    Always ask her where she goes.
    Never trust a dancing daughter,
    Never buy her open clothes.
    Never trust a dancing daughter,
    Don't step on her crooked toes.
    Yeah, yeah, yeah, yeah, yeah, yeah,
    Yeah, yeah, yeah.
    Dancing daughter soon will leave you,
    She will dance right out the door.
    Dancing daughter soon will grieve you,
    And you'll see her nevermore.
    Yeah, yeah, yeah, yeah, yeah, yeah,
    Yeah, yeah, yeah.
    Never trust a dancing daughter,

She'll disturb your sweet repose.
Never trust a dancing daughter,
You'll grow dim the more she glows.
Never trust a dancing daughter,
Lock her out unless it snows.
Yeah, yeah, yeah, yeah, yeah, yeah,
Yeah, yeah, yeah.
Dancing daughter soon will leave you,
She will dance right out the door.
Dancing daughter soon will grieve you,
And you'll see her nevermore.
Yeah, yeah, yeah, yeah, yeah, yeah.

IBOLYA   I don't love you. All I remember is you hollering and screaming ever since I was a baby. I still have the scar on my forehead. Look, look at it! That's what you mean to me. You frighten me and you're cheap. You won't give me any money.

PSCHUG (*Slowly releases her and lifts the hair off her forehead. There is no scar there*)   How can I excuse it? I have hurt you too much! Maybe even your brains fall out when I hit you so hard. Now I read your name with men not in general publication for newlyweds. You are whore and have no religion!

IBOLYA   Sure I have religion. Here . . .
   (*She removes two bobby pins from her hair, crosses them, and hands the cross to* PSCHUG)

PSCHUG   In my extremest yearning I accept the cross in any form. This "in" joke is first sign of hope. I accept . . . but I accept from a stranger. (*Louder, with emotion*) I accept from a stranger, not from Ibolya. I now wish to give that stranger five dollars in passing.

IBOLYA (*Greedily snatching the money*)   Thanks. Now I don't have to kill myself.

PSCHUG   Wait!
   (IBOLYA *continues walking*)

IBOLYA   Aw, shut up!
   (PSCHUG *rushes over to her in a rage and knocks her down.
   She passes out. Blood trickles from the side of her mouth*)

PSCHUG (*He reaches into his shopping bag. He takes out his
   microphone which he puts on*)   I need to amplify my already
   voice! Because God, God don't hear so good!
   (*He shakes fist heavenward.* THE FEDS *surround* IBOLYA
   and accompany her with guitars in a revival-type song)

IBOLYA (*Singing*)
   I'm gonna lie here till I'm born.

THE FEDS (*Singing*)
   She's gonna rise up in the morn.

IBOLYA
   Cause my death is so forlorn.

THE FEDS
   Like a sheep her life's been shorn.

IBOLYA
   How can I, I, I say goodbye?

THE FEDS
   Lord, don't let her say goodbye.
   (THE FEDS *continue strumming their guitars with the same
   theme over and over again, like drums to the guillotine*)

MRS. FRAAK   Oh, I knew this would happen weeks ago. I must
   have been psychic with a telepathic photoflash brain. Why didn't
   I put it into a sealed envelope and send it to the F.B.I.? (*To
   ANDY*) As soon as Dr. Fraak comes to, he'll tell us who drugged
   him, Andy. Stay by him. I'm going to call the police.

ANDY   Keep the narco-bulls out of it. We're all in this together.

MRS. FRAAK (*To* THE FEDS) Who gave you permission to play?
   (THE FEDS *point to each other and continue playing*)

MRS. FRAAK I said—

> (DR. FRAAK *wakes up in an instant and leaps up—very fit and talkative*)

DR. FRAAK So you're all here! The dog, the wife, the father! Well, you have me. You've caught me with my pants down. (*He sees* IBOLYA *lying on the floor*) What's happened? (*He sinks to his knees to examine* IBOLYA) She's in danger. She's very sick. We must get her to a hospital!

PSCHUG No, you not take her out! When she is little girl I think: "If she die now, she become angel. I buy small stone lamb for grave. She go to heaven, be happy." But my wife take her far away where she grow up in sin! Now I want her die in sin. Now she become devil. I buy big stone have no picture—no word— only it stay very heavy on her chest. When I think: "Where Ibolya is?" then I know. I know she is dead. I not shame for her!

DR. FRAAK (*To* THE FEDS) Get him away from the door! I can carry her to the hospital, it's just around the corner. The pressure on her brain must be relieved!

IBOLYA Doc, Doc.

DR. FRAAK Yes, dear.

IBOLYA Doc, you know what to do. I can take it. Drill a hole in my head.

DR. FRAAK I don't know if I can. I haven't performed a trepanning in years. (*Musing*) But I must! (*He starts to rush out*) Don't die till I clean up. I'll be right back. (*He goes out and comes back almost immediately, dressed in a white apron and a cook's cap. He is holding a rotary egg beater. He approaches* IBOLYA *and places the egg beater at her forehead. He revolves it, performing the operation*) How do you feel? That's all there is to it.

IBOLYA I'm high as a kite, and now I even have a place to hide my gum. It's great to be alive!

PSCHUG No. no, go die! Leave me alone. How shall it be. Ah, God, there's none to pity her. Hold your arms to me—climb my neck—kiss me lips to lips. Quick—die! Or I drag myself forever, I drag myself into your lost games. My life is waste, but I warn you! You who hear me now; for I have prophecy! You who are soon to die!

(*He flattens himself even more against the door which he is guarding*)

MRS. FRAAK Mr. Pschug, will you allow me to go? There is no reason to prevent my leaving. You're not as crazy as you seem, are you? None of us is. We're all rational people. Let Andy and me go out that door, and I swear to you my husband will relinquish his hypnotic hold on your daughter. She's just a lamb who's gone astray. Jesus would have forgiven her; allowed her to cook for him, wash his feet. I've been needing a cook myself. If she goes straight, I'll divorce the doctor and take Ibolya in. You can come visit us. You do like me, don't you? Remember what we exchanged? Remember how visual your instruction was? It impressed me! You had vigorous thrust to burn! Let me and Andy go. Please? I have to curb him, he's been indoors too long.

PSCHUG The dog can go. The dog is free.

(ANDY *rushes out of the door that* PSCHUG *holds open just a crack*)

MRS. FRAAK How do you like that! The dog means more to you than I do!

PSCHUG You have no place to go. One woman should be comfort to other woman. Maybe I change my mind. Maybe she not need die in this mortal frame. Is God's business. Go, tell her I disappear. I not be one to strike fatal blow.

MRS. FRAAK (*Kneeling by* IBOLYA) Ibolya, your father says he won't kill you any more. He's going away.

IBOLYA Goodbye. (*Waving to* PSCHUG) *Goodbye.*

DR. FRAAK—Do not disturb the patient. That goes for everyone.

THE FEDS—We're all shook-up. Let us help you Dr. Fraak. We know how to work the sterilizer.

> (*They take the egg beater away from* DR. FRAAK *and put it into the sterilizer*)

DR. FRAAK (*To himself*) Years and years of study and I had to fall asleep on my couch. Thousands of dollars worth of education, and I can't help myself. Well, there is one thing I can do— (*He wearily goes to the phone and dials. He speak into the phone*) Hello—Nurse Brown? Oh, Nurse Linglung—get me Nurse Lattio. *Hello—Lat? Listen—I'm going to do something* rather unprecedented. I have a family problem myself. Someone close to me has gone mental. Yes, extremely mental! All in the head mental. No, not violent. Pathetic. A Parent-pathetic case. Got a pencil? Good, jot this down on your file card. Dr. Toloon-Fraak, diagnosis: bin looney—address—you'll find it in your companion file. Send a car and Dr. Essex Flaesch. I'll go quietly. I've had a nap. Yes, I'm serious. More serious than I've ever been in my life. Take care of that immediately, will you, Lat? Thanks.

MRS. FRAAK You're copping out. You think you can leave the whole thing on my shoulders. Why, that hospital is like a club to you!

THE FEDS Lady, he's a sharp operator; if he commits himself we can't prosecute!

MRS. FRAAK Who are you?

> (THE FEDS *whip off their long wigs; pinned to the inside are detective badges*)

MRS. FRAAK I thought you'd never get here! This entire office including the dressing room, is a Mafia holdout. And that old man is an international spy. His daughter is an international trouble-maker. She's taken my husband away from me and ruined his private practice. She powders her face with heroin and paints her mouth with poppy juice. Dr. Toloon-Fraak, before he went mad, kissed her deeply and licked her lips. Then he put his tongue into her ears which she stuffs with vials of morphine. There is not an inch of Ibolya's body that does not contain some illegal essence. Even I am floating away.

(*She starts to faint.* DR. FRAAK *catches her*)

DR. FRAAK   I think I'll sign her in, too. It'll be like a second honeymoon. We'll meet for socials and make love on the grounds. I might even persuade her to raid the pharmacy with me some night. It's my fault she never had any fun. I plan to change all that if we can synchronize our schedules.

PSCHUG   Me too, Doc. Without Ibolya, I be crazy anyway.

DR. FRAAK   Look, Pschug, that depends on whether there's a bed available. You may have to go on a waiting list.

THE FEDS (*Singing*)
Easy come, easy go,
Easy come, easy go,
Take it easy, take it slow,
Easy come, easy go.

Easy come, easy go,
Easy come, easy go,
We're The Feds and we should know,
Easy come, easy go.
(*A buzzer sounds.* DR. FRAAK *goes to a wall inter-building phone and clicks it on. We can hear a voice over a loudspeaker*)

VOICE   Hello?

DR. FRAAK   Hello.

VOICE   Dr. Fraak?

DR. FRAAK   Speaking.

VOICE   Hi, Toloon, we're waiting for you in the car. What a way to get a free ride! Ha, ha, ha. Hurry down, we're double-parked.

DR. FRAAK Say, Essex, I have two more passengers for you, got room?

VOICE This is an American car, Fraak, not one of those little foreign jobs you race around in. Come on down now, huh?
(DR. FRAAK *clicks off the phone and hangs up the earpiece*)

DR. FRAAK Shall we go, my dear? I want you to listen to whatever I tell you. There is a certain behavior that is required at the hospital, characterized by almost complete acquiescence to the staff in charge. (*They pause at the door*) At first they'll take away personal objects that may prove to be harmful to you, like the microphone, and—(*They exit.* DR. FRAAK *returns for a moment and motions to* PSCHUG) Well, Pschug, what're you waiting for?

PSCHUG Nothing.

DR. FRAAK Well, then, come on.

PSCHUG I cross my fingers, Dr. Fraak. I go with you.
(*They exit.* THE FEDS *start strumming their guitars in an ominous way*)

IBOLYA Say it isn't so! You're not going to book me! I don't believe it. If you take me in, I'll lose faith in the whole human race.
(THE FEDS *lift her up and put her in a chair. She sits sadly, her hair in front of her face. One of* THE FEDS *brushes the hair out of her face*)

THE FEDS (*They serenade her*)
We got a message, baby,
That's gonna kiss your eyes.
We got a message, baby,
That's gonna take the prize.
We dig you so much, baby,
Your income's gonna rise.
So why not come along, strum along, sing along, baby, with
me.

We're gonna book you, baby,
Out of this old terrain.
We're gonna join you, baby,
We're gonna blow your brain.
We dig you so much, baby,
Come on in out of the rain.
So why not come along, strum along, sing along, baby, with
    me.

IBOLYA I'll be a teen-age idol! We'll cut discs together. Travel!
Club dates all over America! Let's call ourselves The Three Feds
and a Head. Or: Three Wills and a Won't! Or . . . oh, I'm so
happy I could fly!

THE FEDS It's your life, and you can fly if you want to.

IBOLYA (*Singing*)
    I'm gonna fly with homemade wings,
    In pretty lace and angel things.
    And when I fly,
    People passing by
    Will know exactly
    What I signify.

    They'll shout: "She's a mountain,
    Like a solid fountain.
    She's a birdlike creature,
    In a full-length feature.
    She's a song of joy,
    And a paper toy,
    And her song is love,
    And her soap is Dove."

    I'm gonna fly with homemade wings,
    In feather boas and rainbow swings.
    And when I fly,
    People passing by
    Won't ask each other
    What I signify.

I'm a medical journal,
I am life eternal.
I'm a bathroom tiled,
Freaking out and wild.
And I want some sex
With tyrannosaurus rex.
If I bite his tail,
I'll send it back by mail.

I'm gonna fly with dragon wings,
And a tongue of fire hung on by wire.
And when I fly,
People passing by
Won't have to ask
What I signify.

'Cause I look like burning
To the Earth returning.
Like a bright white light
On a good trip night.
And I'll build a shrine
To be known as mine.
Rap loud and free
With the god in me.

I'm gonna fly with vinyl wings,
Rain-resistant shiny things.
And when I fly,
People passing by
Will known exactly
What I signify.

Blackout

Home Movies

CAST

MRS. VERDUN
An imposing woman of grandiose proportions. She wears a sweeping lace peignoir over a silk or satin sheath, so that her gestures flow around her. Her ears sparkle with drop diamond earrings and her neck strains beneath a garrote of similar composition. She enjoys herself and others, sexually and conversationally, although pseudo-religiosity is the operational framework.

MR. VERDUN
An exercise nut, appears in running trunks and an athletic shirt marked with the number 11 on the back. He is muscled, limber, and ready to go. He loves his wife, pities his daughter, and controls both.

VIVIENNE
The daughter, a maiden in her thirties. She is homely, zany, and longs to be nude in mixed company. She wears one-piece knickers with a zipper running full length. The knickers are of yellow angora and make her look like a fluffy canary. Beneath this coverall she is wearing a white brassiere with crisp, huge daisies pinned to the cups.

VIOLET
The colored maid, a gorgeous supple beauty, completely at home in her surroundings. All desire her. She wears practically nothing: a top of feathery

petals and a bottom of the same. Her long legs are encased in net stockings and her high-heeled shoes are spiked. Hooked to her bodice is a pom-pom, with which she occasionally dusts furniture and people.

CHARLES   The intellectual; he has a poignant quality. He wears a long scarf made up of patches. On his cheeks consumptive red spots stand out against off-white, clown-like make-up.

PETER   The homosexual, he wears layers of clothing: a jacket, vest, lamé shirt, red dress (to which he finally strips), a head-band, and a necklace. He is innocent, sweet, and full of love—a sympathetic guest.

JOHN   The truck driver, he wears any working outfit, plus a hat. In his pocket is a huge pencil. He shows burlesque dumbness and overt sexuality.

FATHER SHENANAGAN   Dressed as a priest; he has an angelic countenance and perfect pitch. He is a bit of a lecher.

SISTER THALIA   She is in nun habiliment. She wears an awful platinum-blonde wig under her wimple. She has a crush on Father Shenanagan but is hardly aware of it. Nervous as a little mouse. She is a refugee from an Eisenstein movie.

HOME MOVIES *was first presented on May 11, 1964, at the Judson Poets' Theater with the following cast:*

(In order of appearance)

MRS. VERDUN	Gretel Cummings
VIVIENNE	Sudie Bond
VIOLET	Barbara Ann Teer
PETER PETEROUTER	Fredie Herko
SISTER THALIA	Sheindy Tokayer
FATHER SHENANAGAN	Al Carmines
CHARLES ANDUIT	Otto Mjaanes
JOHN THE TRUCKDRIVER	Jim Anderson
MR. VERDUN	George Bartenieff

Directed by Lawrence Kornfeld

Music by Al Carmines

Scene: Behind a curtain is a raked bed, sumptuously covered. To the right of the bed is a small stand, on which sits a bowl of fruit. There is a gaudy backdrop. An upright piano is on the stage.

The curtain opens from left to right. The silence is broken by the sound of FATHER SHENANAGAN *singing Gregorian plainsong. He comes through the curtain, crosses the stage, singing, to the piano. He sits, plays a minor cord, which is sustained as long as possible, and then abruptly swings into lively opening music. One at a time, the actors cross in front of the curtain and go offstage. Their movements are broad, in character, and in burlesque style,* VIOLET *is the last to cross; she opens the curtain on* MRS. VERDUN, *who is lying on the bed as* VIVIENNE *crosses to sit on the piano.* VIOLET *goes offstage, dusting things and* MRS. VERDUN.

MRS. VERDUN   Ever since your father died I have thought of the bliss complete we shared: stared at by the neighbors in envy, as they knew we were continually in love and I was the loveliest of brides, unbridled in a garden filled with divers flowers: none so gay as I.

VIVIENNE   You make me nervous. As if that idiot you married was capable of anything.

MRS. VERDUN   He was never sick a day in his life. He contributed generously to all disease-fighting organizations. He showed no favoritism.

VIVIENNE   Yeah, him and his clean wall crusade. Made a habit of stealing my ink ereaser whenever he went downtown.

MRS. VERDUN   I wish you would hold your tongue, but later, not now. Later, when old friends of your father come to call. I want you to be nice.

VIVIENNE (*She gets off the piano and crosses to* MRS. VERDUN *on the bed*)   Does that mean I have to keep my clothes on again?

MRS. VERDUN   The day had to come. Oh, why do you desire your downfall with such insistence?

VIVIENNE   You know I want to cast out virginity with one fell swoop of the moopem. Why do you always say don't? In the light of the final end we must all pay with our lives.

MRS. VERDUN   You're jumbling. You have a dribbling, indistinct palate, and I will not tolerate that in my house no matter where else it occurs. Understand?

VIVIENNE(*She unzips her knickers to the waist and reveals her breasts; they are encased in a brassiere with daisies sewn on the nipple part*)   What do you think of this, Mums? I grew them yesterday with my own fertilizer. Let me at least show how my garden grows. Don't you think it a sort of miracle: daisy tits that will not wilt without water.
(She examines the daisies closely)

MRS. VERDUN   I ought to horsewhip you with my egg beater, but Aunt Helen borrowed it the other day to make whipped cream for the top of your little cousin Joany's birthday cake. She was six last Friday and enjoyed that fish I sent them for supper. They never eat the body of the Lord in vain.

VIVIENNE   Even though fish have flesh, they're human too. The proof is in the gills.

MRS. VERDUN   The gills?

VIVIENNE   Didin't we used to have them?

MRS. VERDUN   Always the question and the answer. Sometimes the answer and the question. Sometimes the answer. Sometimes the question. And in the end, or at the beginning, a blast of light from the East! Our Lord was born.

VIVIENNE   Mums, you're awful. Remember, I'm religious too. *(She closes the curtain and sings, as the cast behind the curtain sing in counterpoint)*

Glory be to thee, absurdum:
Glory be to thee in admasculum.
Glory to glory in Gloria's glorious and thy ...
A mania.
I would fink and I would be finked.
I would smear and I would be smeared.
I would be bought, being hole and nought,
Being whole and nought,
A mania.
Crap danceth. I would crap. Crap ye all. A mania.
Wherefool I lay, loose walls decay: lament ye all.
A mania.
　　(VIVIENNE *opens the curtain*)
The number twelve is on the shelve ... (*To* MRS. VERDUN) Shall
I continue?

MRS. VERDUN　Haven't you forgotten something?

VIVIENNE　Let's see. Oh yes. (*As the chorus sings again, she
chants*)　Ad infinitum, ad infinitum menstrualis, menstrualis
corpus Christi, finiculus umbilicalis.

MRS. VERDUN　Later I expect you to express your devotions with
emphasis on Vesica Urinaria, your patron saint.

VIVIENNE　He achieved sainthood in such a lovely way ... (*She
pantomimes washing*) his huge male hands up to the elbows in
soapy water, scrubbing the underwear of those village women,
while they jeered and brought him fresh supplies.

MRS. VERDUN　I don't think it's Christian of you to spread rumors.
　　(VIOLET, *the maid, enters; she wears practically nothing*)

VIOLET　Someone to see you, m'am. So you get up offen the bed
and let me make it. I wish you wouldn't stay in bed all the time.
There's an awful fusty odor in here. I think I g'wine open the
windows.

MRS. VERDUN　Don't you dare take such decisions on yourself. But
yes, of course, open the windows. Wait, I don't want them

opened too wide. No, that's too wide. Lower them. (*During these instructions regarding the windows,* VIOLET *lowers and raises her breasts as she would the window*) Remember, if you don't understand how we do things here in New York, back you'll go, back where you came from. Virginia, I believe!

VIOLET Yeah!

MRS. VERDUN You must say yes, not yeah, unless it's at the end of a prayer, Violet. Yes?

VIOLET You gettin' up, or should I entertain the company?

MRS. VERDUN Who, may I ask, has arrived?

VIOLET A young gennulman call Peter Peterouter. He's wearin' my favorite perfume, "White Shoulders." It never comes true though.

MRS. VERDUN Perhaps it will when you visit Lourdes.

VIOLET Lords? And ladies too? They old friends of your husband, m'am?

MRS. VERDUN Oh, I have to explain everything to you, wooly head. I mean the miraculous Lourdes where miracles *do* happen. I might take us all there in time. It depends.

VIOLET You wouldn't take li'l ole me fresh fum de sharecroppers' cottage shack where I was born.

MRS. VERDUN You know very well I couldn't do without you, Violet. So don't pull that ole darky act on me. There was a time when I would have ignored your education, but now, of course, I realize your possibilities. (MRS. VERDUN *rises from the bed, her peignoir floating behind her.* VIVIENNE *jumps on the bed and stretches out on it*) Please tell me in as short a time as you can how many by-products the peanut has.

VIOLET (*Singing; also burlesqueing a sexy walk, with bumps and grinds*)
Peanut oil, peanut butter,
Salted cocktail peanuts,
Peanut in the shell,
Peanut brittle. . .

MRS. VERDUN (*Interrupting*) I knew you were an heiress when I hired you. That's why your pay is so minimal.

VIOLET (*Continuing*)
. . . peanut cookies, peanut synthetic fabric, and peanut ice cream.

MRS. VERDUN At the same time I respect your future. You can pick up the clothes later. Better make the bed first. (*She throws* VIVIENNE *off the bed and gets back on it.* VIVIENNE *goes behind* MRS. VERDUN *and plays with her hair in an ill-tempered manner*) And when you're done with that see if my gargling glass has dried toothpaste on it. I was disgusted with the condition of my own individual glass yesterday and had to cup water into my mouth with my hands instead of using my own gargling glass which should be kept immaculate because not only did I buy it especially at the exclusive bathroom shop at Saks Fifth Avenue for my own use because it had my initials embossed in gold on it, but what was I saying?

VIOLET You sayed dat your mouf smell.

MRS. VERDUN I didn't hire you for your sense of humor. I'm completely aware of the race hatred you bear me . . . (*She goes to* VIOLET *and embraces her*) but I embrace and love you like a little child who is spontaneous to the point of complete exhaustion and must be put bodily to bed in the middle of the game no matter who's losing.

VIOLET (*Moving away from* MRS. VERDUN) I'm glad you 'preciate my efforts, otherwise there'd be no recompense. No recompense,

wreck-um-pants, pants-um-wreckum. (*She mouths the words, fascinated, studying the sound*)
Wreck-um-pants
Pants-um-wreckum

BOTH (*They sing this four or five times as they meet at center stage*)
Wreck-um-pants
Pants-um-wreckum

VIVIENNE (VIVIENNE *closes the curtain behind them. She imitates* VIOLET) Peanut ice cream.

VIOLET I'm glad you 'preciate my efforts.

MRS. VERDUN Yes, I do. Now take these clothes and put them in the cleaners, dear, and when you go down please see whether Vivienne's other knickers have come back yet. I reminded them on Wednesday that I wanted them on Thursday, and now it's Friday and I don't think they'll have them till next Tuesday. They're so unreliable.

VIOLET (*Chewing gum vigorously*) Yes'm. Shall I announce your appearance into the other room where that strange friend of your missing husbin' is waiting for you?

MRS. VERDUN Get rid of that gum. Get rid of it. Do you hear? Rid-of-it. It's not becoming for a maid of your age and position to talk and chew at the same time. One would think you were a cow chewing cud. (VIOLET *leaves.* MRS. VERDUN *speaks to the audience*) She does resemble a cow pat, or turd drying in the good Lord's sun.
(*She exits*)

VIVIENNE (*Enters with a Bible*) Ma. (*Pause*) Ma. (*Pause*) Ma! (*Pause.* MRS. VERDUN *enters*) You forgot this again, Ma.

MRS. VERDUN Thank you, dear.
(*She takes the Bible and exits*)

VIVIENNE (*Alone, in front of the curtain*)
   I would fink and I would be finked.
   I would smear and I would be smeared.
   I would be bought, being hole and nought,
   Being whole and nought,
   A mania.
      (VIVIENNE *opens the curtain and exits.* MRS. VERDUN *and*
      PETER *are discovered sitting on the bed.* PETER *is ensconced*
      at one end, MRS. VERDUN *at the other*)

MRS. VERDUN   I think fruit is so nice in the summer, don't you?

PETER   Oh yes, I adore fruit in the summer.

MRS. VERDUN   So refreshing.

PETER   Succulent.

MRS. VERDUN   Ripe.

PETER   Juicy!

MRS. VERDUN   Dripping.

PETER   Ever so wet.

MRS. VERDUN   Would you care for a fruit?

PETER   But your bowl is so delightful to look at, I wouldn't dream
   of disturbing the arrangement. If, of couurse, you have more in
   the kitchen . . . I prefer peaches.

MRS. VERDUN   As soon as my maid is free, she'll serve us.

PETER   No hurry. I like waiting for my pleasures. Often, you
   know, the expectation is better than the realization. Although,
   when you have one in the hand, why wait for two in the bush?

MRS. VERDUN (*Singing*)
   All birdies fly away;

Even those you've had in the hand.
Nothing seems to keep winged creatures
From using their wings.
Away they go.
Away into the wild blue yonder.
All birdies fly away,
All birdies fly away,
Even those, even those you've had in the hand.
   (*She jumps off the bed, crosses to the apron of the stage and belts out a repeat of the song to the audience*)

PETER   Fruits are the same; once eaten, they are gone forever, and the gas pains they cause flutter and fuss inside like wings.
   (MRS. VERDUN *drags* PETER *downstage, where they sing*)

MRS. VERDUN
   Like wings aloft,
   Caught in an intestinal updraft.

PETER
   Like wings aloft,
   Caught in an intestinal updraft.

MRS. VERDUN
   It's true dear,
   That if something else
   Is caught in the whirl
   Of something else entirely,
   It just can't help itself,
   But must continue
   In the powerful current
   Of that particular thing.

PETER
   Yes, we just can't help it;
   The route we go,
   A power stronger than will.

BOTH
   It just can't help itself,

But must continue
In the powerful current
Of that particular thing.
A Godlike power,
Completely invisible.
The route we go,
A power stronger than will.

PETER

A power stronger than will.

MRS. VERDUN

A power stronger than will.

BOTH

A power stronger than will.

PETER (*He slumps back*)   Till the explosion, then BOOM! Everything gives way and falls into small portions. Sometimes I think the good Lord created everything by chance, set off the cherry bomb and waited for the shapes to crack.

MRS. VERDUN   Your attitude reminds me of my husband, who said anything he pleased.

PETER   He was a fine man.

MRS. VERDUN   Yes.

PETER   Strong.

MRS. VERDUN   Exceedingly muscled.

PETER   Well hung.

MRS. VERDUN   What was that?

PETER   His deportment in private excited my deepest admiration.

MRS. VERDUN Where was it you two met? I thought it a coincidence that he should bring you home after I was already so familiar with your mother who visits me often to chat.

PETER (*Singing*)
Mother told me about you,
And then I told her about the gymnasium
Where I met him.
    (*He turns to the audience*)
He was rather close-lipped.
I didn't know him well, although
We used the equipment together.
It was an inner feeling that we felt,
An unspoken man-to-man sympathy
Based on the fact that we spent so much time there.
Any overture would have spoiled
The innocent childlike aura
    (*On his knee*)
Of our relationship.
(*He falls back to the floor in a languid pose*)

MRS. VERDUN Now that he's gone I suppose the truth has dawned.

PETER A terrible truth covered with the rash . . .

MRS. VERDUN But physical discomforts concern me not. (*She speaks while sentimental music plays in the background*) I believe in the hereafter. I believe in a vast wooly tomb shaded from without, by huge striped awnings flapping in the wind like wings. I believe my husband's soul is a lost crow frightened forever by the motion of those awnings.
    (*The music stops*)

PETER He is not a man to take limbo lying down, but in love and death we all lean back to die.

MRS. VERDUN He had one thing which concerned him above all else.

PETER Yes?

MRS. VERDUN He wanted his daughter Vivienne to marry a suitable gentleman of his acquaintance.

PETER If she resembles him I'd be interested.

MRS. VERDUN She resembles him in character, but her fine points are as unrealized as a tadpole's. She looks a bit like you. Let me see, turn to the side. Ah yes, there you are.

PETER Here I am, and I'd like to meet her, but you might as well know that although Oscar Wilde had children . . .

MRS. VERDUN The author?

PETER Do you know any other?

MRS. VERDUN No.

PETER That although he had children he was not quite suitable. Like myself, he held a part of himself back for others, strangers who could never bear the fruit of his seed.

MRS. VERDUN Perhaps you are right. To be turgid under cover of darkest night is not the whole story. He might have been dreaming of those strangers at the very time he was planting those seeds.

PETER (*Speaking over sentimental music*) The opalescent dew of his desire, as mine, was drawn by three black stallions wearing emerald ostrich plumes and jeweled trappings. Some might call it queer, but the natural aristocrat finds it a most usual way to travel.
   (*The music stops*)

MRS. VERDUN Who's an aristocrat these days?
   (*She sighs*)

PETER I am. Watch me metamorph into a mannered and pompous queen. Discount my suit and call me Caladonia. Then ask me, "Caladonia, Caladonia, what makes your big head so hard?"

MRS. VERDUN If I ask you, "Caladonia, Caladonia, what makes your big head so hard?" will you answer me?

PETER I'll demonstrate.

MRS. VERDUN Caladonia, you may begin.
> (*To rhythmic strip music,* PETER *takes off his jacket, his pants, his shoes; he wraps his tie around his head like a bandanna, puts on a rhinestone necklace, lowers his red shirt, which is in fact a dress, to his knees. Having completed his metamorphosis into a "pompous queen," he prances around, making grotesque faces to the audience.* MRS. VERDUN *coughs to get his attention. The music changes to "All Birdies Fly Away" as* PETER *closes the curtain in front of him, looking at the audience with a sweet, innocent face. There is a brief pause; then* VIVIENNE *enters. They look at each other, startled, then sing*)

VIVIENNE (*Singing*)
> You look like me.
> If I had a brother, he would look like you.
> Would you like to come and live with me?

PETER (*Singing*)
> You look the way I'd have looked
> If I had been a girl.
> You are my female counterpane.
> > (PETER *and* VIVIENNE *repeat the song, this time singing simultaneously*)

BOTH
> I'll bet we could tell each other secrets,
> And find each other sweethearts.

VIVIENNE
> And eat each other's leftovers.

PETER
> And wear each other's underwear.

BOTH
> And play catch as catch can.

VIVIENNE Not in my bunny slippers. I wouldn't do that in them. The ears rip off too easy in my bunny slippers. I might try Graeco-Roman in them but never ketch-ez-ketch kan. I hate to sew the damn things on. When I trip on them I break my glasses and that blinds me temporarily.

PETER Oh, I'm so sorry. You're much too nice a lady to go blind temporarily. One would think there'd be special dispensation for the good people; for the really good ones, so that tragedies didn't happen to them all the time. If I was your brother I'd never cause you pain or blindness. I'd fall first.

VIVIENNE The first fall is the fall from grace. After that nothing matters because who cares?

PETER Nobody cares but mothers. Mothers do care, you know.
> (MRS. VERDUN *enters*)

VIVIENNE (*Singing*)
> My mother wears a concave lens.
> She has trouble focusing.
> For years I hated her because
> I thought her squint was an expression of evil.
>
> Remember when I hated you
> And you loved me in spite of it?
> I thought she was putting the curse on me.
> Isn't that right, Mamma? Didn't I hate you?

MRS. VERDUN My little girl has always adored me. She wears concave lenses. For years I believed that I hated her, held her responsible for the looks we gave each other, but she had weak eyes too. We all have weak eyes. But it doesn't matter because . . . (*She sings*)
> Once you've seen everything,
> What is there to see?
> My olfactory sense

Has sharpened, though,
Sharpened so.
We all have weak eyes
But it doesn't matter.
No, it doesn't matter because
Once you've seen everything,
What is there to see?
My olfactory sense
Has sharpened, though,
Sharpened so.

For instance, I can identify that perfume you're wearing. It's "White Shoulders," isn't it?

(VIVIENNE *opens the curtain*)

PETER   I'm wearing "White Shoulders" on top, but underneath there's still the lingering odor of "Bagatelle." It expresses the real me.

MRS. VERDUN (*She approaches* CHARLES, *who is standing behind the bed*)   I wasn't familiar with "Bagatelle," but now that we're acquainted, my nose will not play tricks. Peter, I want you to meet Charles Anduit. He writes books. My, my, an author. I've always wanted to write myself, but I've been written already. Pleased to meet you, Charles. I hope we'll get to know each other better as the evening progresses.

VIOLET (*After* CHARLES *whispers to her*)   Mistah Chas. say dat if you don' stop suckin' you friggin' lips in like you doin', he goin' to sew dem up wif de topmast fum a model schooner. Ain' dat a scream.

VIVIENNE (*She reveals a daisied breast*)   I thought you came here to see me. Daddy had it arranged.

VIOLET (*After* CHARLES *whispers to her*)   Mistah Chas. say dat no frigit dike goin' tell him whose nooky ta tickle. He say dat when he do you all de favah of his company, he thank you all kindly to shut up. And, he want more to eat. And he say send de fairy to de kitchen for anothah peach, pronto!

(PETER *goes to the kitchen, making a big display of his good nature. He smiles, swishes, pirouettes*)

MRS. VERDUN Charles dear, I know you think of me as an old cow, but time is running out and I must know. Is a woman's brain smaller than a man's?

VIOLET (*After* CHARLES *whispers to her*) Woman's is got a more rounder an' shinier skull wat a man's got, but spite a dat news de truth is dat both is infinite-dismal. However, de proportions is jest right. Dat is to say, he ain't g'wine put down de chick brain wave in any sense, since however even the inferior wall outside of Jerusalem.

VIVIENNE (*She starts to undress, but her zipper jams*) Damn, damn, damn, damn it to hell. I should have installed a new improved zipper that meshes and unmeshes at a touch. Can't even undress peacefully in my own home.

VIOLET (*After* CHARLES *whispers to her*) Chas. say dat he got a putty good idee wut you got fum past performance, but he glad you attemptin' it again cause it give you kicks and evybody should get dey kicks.

VIVIENNE You can tell Chas. that he always spoils my fun. (CHARLES *gets up and grabs* VIVIENNE. *He kisses her wildly, passionately, sadistically*) Oh! oh! How voracious you are. Charles, I dislike you intensely. (*Choking him*) Say that you love me.

VIOLET (*After* CHARLES *whispers to her*) He say dat he love you, dat you de fox fo him. But he promised you mothah fust, me secunt, and he want to try de pansy too, but you can come along as de lookout.

VIVIENNE If only father were here. Life is so weird without him. (*There is a knock on the door.* JOHN, *a huge truckman, pushes a large wooden closet onto the stage. It has tags on it and a mirror the length of its door*)

JOHN Who'll sign for this?

MRS. VERDUN I will, young man. Bring your bill of lading here. Father Shenanagan is expected any moment with Sister Thalia. Did you happen to see a short father with a medium sister outside my door?

JOHN Them people answer your description are downstairs in the lobby. Couldn't all fit in the elevator.

MRS. VERDUN Good. They've come to comfort me. I'm receiving calls of condolence on the disappearance of my husband. We haven't seen or heard from him for a month of Sundays. T. God for ceremony; it fills in the gaps.

JOHN Gee, lady, I hate to do a stupid thing like deliver a closet at a time like this.

MRS. VERDUN We must proceed normally if we are to retain a modicum of sanity, must we not? Think of it, one never knows who's going next these days.

JOHN No truer words were spoken, lady. I spoke, lady, once—and it was no truer.

MRS. VERDUN What a beautiful closet it is, so ample, and the mirror goes up and down, up and down. (*Stepping back so that she bumps into* JOHN) Excuse me.

JOHN Ample it is. Holds five suits, six dresses, four hats, one umbrella, two pairs of slippers, and four pairs of shoes.

MRS. VERDUN Does it? How marvelous. You know your stock well.

JOHN Yeah, an it comes with a six-month guarantee.

MRS. VERDUN What could possibly happen to this?
          (*She caresses the closet*)

JOHN If the mirror breaks, we replace it, and if the shelf don't fit, we adjust the fit.

MRS. VERDUN You adjust the fit? All by yourself?

JOHN On company time, Mrs. Trained to do the job.

MRS. VERDUN I'll bet you're an expert.

JOHN I am a bit of an expert on the side.

MRS. VERDUN What side?

JOHN Paternal.

MRS. VERDUN Do you have a pencil?

JOHN Sure. Here you are.
(*He draws a huge, phallic pencil from his pocket*)

MRS. VERDUN Ah, the regalia and adornments of your trade.

JOHN The customer's always right.

MRS. VERDUN I know I'm not wrong about you. I have a feeling in my bones.

JOHN (*He puts his hand in his pocket*) I don't feel any bones.

MRS. VERDUN Give it time. What's your name?

JOHN John.

MRS. VERDUN Give it time, John.

JOHN You say my name as if you like it.

MRS. VERDUN I could like it even more.

JOHN What should I do to make you like it more without endangering my job?

MRS. VERDUN   Be sweet to me. Stay sweet to me. And adjust the price of the closet.

JOHN   Oh, I can't do that, lady. There are duplicates of the bill.

MRS. VERDUN   Just teasing. There is no love without danger, though.

JOHN   I guess I'm too careful in my life for love.

MRS. VERDUN   But you deliver a pretty wild closet.

PETER   (*Returns from the kitchen with a bowl of fruit*)   Fruit, anyone?
　　　　(*There is a blackout*)

VOICE OF MR. VERDUN (*Singing*)
　　　There is nothing wrong with darkness,
　　　Nothing wrong with smells,
　　　But when the darkness has a smell of its own,
　　　And that smell is human,
　　　Then I say let there be light!
　　　If you hear me out there.
　　　Why am I here?
　　　What did I do?
　　　I never did a thing
　　　That didn't need doing
　　　On a small scale.
　　　That didn't need doing
　　　On a small scale.
Why am I confined at the expense of the state I am suffering under? Delusion, all is diluted. That may be my fault, Father, but we share the blame. (*Singing*)
　　　You and I,
　　　She and I,
　　　Us and we,
　　　And those who are no longer citizens.
　　　Wife, where are you?
　　　Where?
　　　I could swear

That I heard whispering and titterings.
Where are they now?
Where is she now?
Answer me someone. I swear it will go badly with you all if I have to break this expensive new closet to get out. I am the victim of a conspiracy. Daughter—wife—friends—
(*He continues knocking and scraping resignedly. The light on the closet dims. The lights go up on* SISTER THALIA *and* FATHER SHENANAGAN, *who are sitting at a kitchen table. Their hands are in a prayerful attitude, catching cockroaches. A competitive cockroach-catching game!*)

FATHER SHENANAGAN   Sister Thalia, how many do you have? I have three.

SISTER THALIA   I have five.

FATHER SHENANAGAN   Do they tickle?

SISTER THALIA   Only when they climb up the sides.

FATHER SHENANAGAN   Do they do that?

SISTER THALIA   Yes indeed, as the good Lord intended.

FATHER SHENANAGAN   Ah, the good Lord for all.

SISTER THALIA   Blessed be the virgin.

FATHER SHENANAGAN   And the virgin forests holding back the floods.

SISTER THALIA   They're disastrous.

FATHER SHENANAGAN   Floods always are, my dear, but the good Lord provides.

SISTER THALIA   In his infinite wisdom.

FATHER SHENANAGAN Thank the Lord for doughnuts and coffee too.

SISTER THALIA I cried when the men protested that my doughnuts were stale.

FATHER SHENANAGAN We must praise the day-old bakery, not condemn it. How many do you have now? I have six.

SISTER THALIA I have four. One got away.

FATHER SHENANAGAN I feel very comfortable in the kitchen, the heart of the home.

SISTER THALIA Oh, oh help me, another got away. I have three. They're all so agile today, I'm sure to lose.

FATHER SHENANAGAN There is no better way to learn humility, Sister Thalia. I have eight.

SISTER THALIA I'm going to let them all go.

FATHER SHENANAGAN Not so soon.

SISTER THALIA I must. They are crawling over the insides of my hands and I've already squashed two accidentally. I concede the victory to you.

FATHER SHENANAGAN And the prize?

SISTER THALIA I will say a prayer for you.

FATHER SHENANAGAN And what else?

SISTER THALIA And let you have some of our home-made wine.

FATHER SHENANAGAN Good, good. It all sounds so very excellent and admirable.

SISTER THALIA It's only fair.

FATHER SHENANAGAN What shall I do with them?

SISTER THALIA Let them run, dear Father, back under the table and into the silverware drawer.

FATHER SHENANAGAN You once promised me a wonderful sight. What is it?

SISTER THALIA Yes I did.

FATHER SHENANAGAN You did promise.

SISTER THALIA I did.

FATHER SHENANAGAN You did.

SISTER THALIA I?

FATHER SHENANAGAN You.

SISTER THALIA It couldn't have been me.

FATHER SHENANAGAN Then who?

SISTER THALIA Number two.

FATHER SHENANAGAN Not you?

SISTER THALIA No.

FATHER SHENANAGAN Dear Sister, you are fibbing. Come, gentle Sister, show me it. (*He sings*)
  Showing is part of penance, you know.
  The more you suffer
  The more He'll understand you.
  Don't be a shy bride.
  Your secretive nature will be protected.
  Fear not.
  I merely want to be

Filled with wonder.
Show me, show me, show me, show me. Oh, I do so want you
To show me the horrible sight.

SISTER THALIA   If you insist.
(SISTER THALIA *removes her wimple, revealing awful platinum-blonde hair. He takes her by the shoulders and presses
her to her knees*)

FATHER SHENANAGAN   Now we must pray together.
(*They pray.* PETER *enters*)

PETER   Business before pleasure, Father? (FATHER SHENANAGAN,
startled, gives him an ugly look that softens into benignity) Well,
anyway, I always feel better when there's a servant of God
around. Speaking of servants, I'm a little serving maid today.

FATHER SHENANAGAN   Please continue what you were doing. I'm
sure you're a comfort and a help.

PETER   I should say so. If it weren't for me this kitchen would be
a real Grand Central Station. And you know, Mrs. Verdun is
in such deep suffering that even she hardly realizes it. Why, to
look at her you'd swear nothing had happened. I suppose it's a
symptom of temporary insanity.

FATHER SHENANAGAN   Yes and no. Sometimes her behavior is
permanent. She languishes wholeheartedly. Her giddy nature
longs to appear seraphic. Her desire is to humble herself before
personal disasters that would make any ordinary Christian die
of shame or chagrin.

PETER   What are those personal disasters that would make any
ordinary Christian die of shame?

FATHER SHENANAGAN   I am not free to divulge—

PETER   What has been whispered in the sacristy?
(SISTER THALIA *struggles up from her knees.* FATHER SHE-

NANAGAN *tries to prevent her from rising. He cannot tear himself away from the vision of her hair*)

SISTER THALIA   When was the last time you bought a candle, dear sir?

PETER   It was at a time, Sister, when I was going through one of those personal disasters, the kind Father Shenanagan will not discuss. It's true, I was ashamed. Ashamed and simply disgusted with myself. So I went to confession. You know, in my parish there are one or two rather adorable young priests. I prefer the chubby amorous ones with stars in their eyes, to the rotten epileptic scapegoats one adamantly associates with true religion. I like to imagine ... well, I can't actually go into that. But the way they conspire with you behind that fancy grillwork. So many things happen to the spirit during confession. I swear I'm reluctant to come to the end of sinful recitation. I have to prevent myself from following those sacred, clinging, flowing gowns on their way to the study. I absolutely rankle in a mad funk when I leave the church; dusty-kneed and on the point of a seizure of love. I've been on that moot point too often. Is it any wonder I take the candle with me?
     (*He disappears under the curtain*)

SISTER THALIA   I believe I should retire to the living room.
     (*She exits,* MR. VERDUN *breaks his way out of the closet, prances around, then sings*)

MR. VERDUN
     Oh my number is eleven on the cross-country run.
     They say the war is over and we've driven out the Hun.
     But seeing is believing and I'll bet you one to one,
     That if anyone is crazy it's my wife, Mrs. Verdun.
     (MRS. VERDUN *screams behind the curtain.* MR. VERDUN *stands up and poses. He makes muscles, faces, examines his legs, loosens the calves, etc.*) Sounds like my dear wife can't take it. I always told her that misery would befall her if I ever kicked the bucket. Boy, was I right. She thinks I jumped off the George Washington Bridge on my way to Jersey during my daily constitutional.

Keep in shape, that's my advice. I'm in shape. What more could she want? She's safe with me. (*He sings*)

> I can save a friend from drowning,
> Wrestle alligators,
> Lift five cows on my shoulders
> With the help of a specially constructed platform.
> Women admire me for my nonchalent bravado,
> But I suspect that Mrs. V.
> Doubts my masculine veracity.

Funny thing happened to me in a health food store the other day. I was ordering my macrobiotic staples from a very healthy looking blonde, so I ventured a stab in the dark, so to speak. As she handed me my package I said: "Baby, I know you sell it, but do you eat it?" and she answered me in a very straightforward health food way. She said: "Listen buster, I can wipe the floor with you, and I have a good mind to do it, dirty slob!" "Stop!" I cried, "You must be a physical culturist too." (*He sings*)

> I know you sell it, but do you eat it?
> I know you sell it, but do you eat it?
> I know you sell it, but do you eat it?
> I know you sell it, but do you eat it?
> You must be a physical culturist,
> You must be a physical culturist,
> You must be a physical culturist too!

SISTER THALIA   I hear a familiar voice.

FATHER SHENANAGAN   Indeed it rings a knell.

SISTER THALIA   It couldn't be.

MR. VERDUN   It is. I. I have returned. I almost went to Hoboken, but habit prevented me from making the trip. How come no one heard me knocking, knocking on the closet door? Are all the deaf in league?

FATHER SHENANAGAN   We were in the kitchen or we would have heard you. We would certainly have heard you if we had been nearby.

MR. VERDUN Enough, you sirrah! I believe you are the eminence I used to hear compound on the dais of a most holy lectern during masses. I always excuse reverent personages in case they put the nix on heaven when I go all the way. Here's my hand, sir, to cement your former usefulness and a low bow to you, sirrah, and a speedy sign of the cross.

SISTER THALIA Bless us all. You echo your own sentiments. I'm afraid to see your wife when she sees you. Solace is a poor substitute for solstice when the sun is set.

PETER (*Recitative*)
 Here they come now.
 I hear a rush of people and a sound of shock which is silence.
 Here they come now;
 About to enter,
 Almost here,
 Cold,
 Warm,
 Warmer,
 Hot, hot, hot,
 Oh burning.
 They have arrived *en masse*.
 Quel avec pomme de terre,
 Mr. Verdun you are discovered.
  (PETER *opens the curtain on the tableau.* MRS. VERDUN *sees* MR. VERDUN *and screams. Then she rushes forward and kisses him loudly. She then pulls a switch and turns white with anger*)

MRS. VERDUN *You* had the gall to readjust my calm routine!

MR. VERDUN If I hadn't ever called you my little pumpkin, I'd say I was remiss, but since I have used endearments often I'd say you're being hard on me.

ALL (*Singing*)
 Being hard on him.

MRS. VERDUN   Ask Charles Anduit who's right or wrong. He has the answer book.

MR. VERDUN   Charles Anduit, that pale-faced, pasty-skinned, moon glow of a masculate?

VIOLET (*After* CHARLES *whispers to her*)   Three cheers for Mr. Verdun. Long may he pursue the iron game and be away fum home so that I, Charles Anduit, may commit daring acts of passion under his very nose, with his wife, daughter, and maid Violet. Welcome home.

MR. VERDUN   Watch out. I speak softly and carry a big stick.
(*He menaces* CHARLES *and they scuffle ineffectually*)

MRS. VERDUN (*She sings as* MR. VERDUN *threatens* CHARLES *and finally knocks him down—a Mack Sennet fight*)
Beat him up. He's a bad boy.
He's boyish and bothersome.
Lower the boom.
Lower the boom.
He deserves a crushing blow.
He took advantage of me.
I cried when he forced me.
'Cause he's so boyish and bothersome.
Lower the boom.
Lower the boom.
Lower the boom.
Lower the boom.
He took advantage of me!
(MRS. VERDUN *sits on* CHARLES *on the last line of her song*)

VIOLET (*Stuttering for* CHARLES)   Help, help, let me up. Please kind mistress.

MRS. VERDUN   I am still capable of largesse, and do not mean to smother you, young youth. Allow me.
(*She helps him up*)

VIOLET   What we is cravin' is soup, and I is got some in de kitchen.
(VIOLET *goes out to bring in the soup.* VIOLET *appears
immediately*)

MR. VERDUN   What kind is it? Answer me. I'm the master here.

VIOLET   Chicken soup with knaidlach.

MRS. VERDUN   Thank God it's not cabbage soup.

VIVIENNE   Or wonton.

VIOLET   Or boy-ya-best.

JOHN   Or borscht.

VIVIENNE   Or pee soup.

PETER   Or dehydrated beef noodle.

FATHER SHENANAGAN   Really thankful that it's not black bean.

SISTER THALIA   Or pee soup.

VIVIENNE   I've already said that.
(*She smacks* SISTER THALIA *on the forehead*)

SISTER THALIA   But I agree. Pee soup is thick green slime. Of
course I'd eat it if the Lord prescribed it in his Canticles of Vir-
tuous Foods.

FATHER SHENANAGAN   That deserves a responsory, but I'd rather
let the Pope in his extraordinary Pallium rule on it. I am merely
a rough-hewn cornerstone. Cujus pulchritudinem.

MRS. VERDUN   I'm going to have some right now.

VIOLET (*After* CHARLES *whispers to her*)   Soup of the evening,
beeootiful soup. (PETER *takes a bowl of soup and hands out soup*

to all the people. Each takes out a soup plate and spoon. They all slurp soup. When PETER *offers* VIOLET *some soup, she morosely brushes him away, takes the stool, plunks it on the apron of the stage, and sits on it. The cast freezes in mid-soup.* VIOLET *confides to the audience; she sings)*

Sometimes I feel like a chocolate turkey
Gazing out of cellophane windows.
Sometimes I feel like I'm almost melted
In the summertime of my race.
Sometimes I feel that my body is hollow,
A long, long way from the mold.
Is there anybody here that's like weepin' Mary?
I'll tell you what the Lord has done for me,
Nothin', nothin', nothin', hallelujah.
That's what the Lord has done for me.
Ask not what the Lord has done for you.
Ask what you can do for your Lord.
Is there anybody here that's like weepin' Mary?
I'll tell you what the Lord has done for me,
Nothin', nothin', nothin', hallelujah.
That's what the Lord has done for me.
Well, ah has to go to de kitchen.

      (She goes. CHARLES *follows her out)*

VIVIENNE *(Singing)*

No one wants to pluck my daisies.
Everyone is fooled by my knickers and glasses.
No one wants to pluck my daisies.
I wonder why?
I grew them yesterday
With my own fertilizer.
Let me at least
Show how my garden grows.
No one wants to pluck my daisies.
Everyone is fooled by my knickers and glasses.

MR. VERDUN Now, now, daughter. You are my very own daughter, and as such I cannot and will not accept the notion that you are strange or ugly. Your knickers are functional. You can stand on your head without embarrassment to anyone. It is not your fault that you are white, and Violet exotic. Charles is best forgotten. He is a fakerino with a farina complexion. He has a marked stutter accompanied by unusual sensitivity of the stuffed derma. He sleeps all day and rides the ferries by night. Altogether not a pretty picture himself.

VIVIENNE   Daddy, how did you guess that I love him?

MR. VERDUN   No mind is the criteria, but mind is ever present. I use my brains.

MRS. VERDUN   (*From behind the curtain*)   What a delicious soup.

VIVIENNE   I'm going to the kitchen to see what Charles and Violet are up to. Why, oh why, did he choose Violet to speak for him? I could have been so understanding, so voluble for his voice, so additive to his meaning, and so kind. I've always wanted the opportunity to be kind. Nobody has ever trusted me with their ailment. I wonder why. (*Singing*)
   No one wants to pluck my daisies.
   Everyone is fooled by my knickers and glasses.
   No one wants to pluck my daisies.
   I wonder why?
      (*She exits.* MRS. VERDUN *enters*)

MRS. VERDUN   See what you've done, you've alienated our daughter.

MR. VERDUN   How?

MRS. VERDUN   Damaging thoughts, they add up. You're responsible.

MR. VERDUN   I accept. Mea Culpa, but who's the busy seamstress with one pattern in her repertoire—knickers?

MRS. VERDUN   My speciality is sportswear; I do what I do best.

MR. VERDUN Something more seductive on the girl might change her life. Get her an invite to the movies at least: give her doddering precursors a shot at each other in privacy. She's always around complaining like a simp; what kind of romantic atmosphere is that for us, dearest? God, how I miss you. (*He starts for her*) My hormones are in top form.

MRS. VERDUN That's the way I like it.

MR. VERDUN (*Singing*)
Beat her up.

MRS. VERDUN (*Singing*)
He's a bad boy.

MR. VERDUN
She's girlish and bothersome.

BOTH
Lower the boom.
Lower the boom.

MRS. VERDUN
He deserves a crushing blow.

MR. VERDUN
I took advantage of her.

MRS. VERDUN
He took advantage of me.

MR. VERDUN
I took advantage of her.

MRS. VERDUN
He'll take advantage of me.

BOTH
(You)
(I) deserve a crushing blow.

Lower the boom.

Lower the boom.

(*As they sing "Lower the boom" over and over again, they go behind the curtain. The full cast joins the singing. The tempo picks up, as* CHARLES *chases* VIVIENNE *past the curtain a few times—a farce chase. They are stopped by* MR. VER-DUN, *who holds* CHARLES *at arm's length*)

MR. VERDUN (*Singing*)

Do not bruise the fruit.

Do not bruise the fruit.

Do not bruise the fruit

That my wife bore and I planted.

Do not expose the pit of that overripe production, or it will dry and become sere. (*Singing*)

It is the pit that holds the bitter almond.

The pit that keeps within it the true soft pit. Do not expose its surface to the breath you exhale and the teeth you dig with. (*Singing*)

Let it lie!

Let it lie!

Let it be half-hard, underripe, green, and about to be. (*Singing*)

Don't feel how soft it is.

Don't bruise the fruit.

Don't bruise the fruit!

Smell it, if you must, (*Singing*)

But don't lay your nose on it.

Let it stay in the basket till it gets rotten and frothy with mold and clings to others in the basket. Yes, let the fruit get rotten without help from your alien hands, Charles Anduit. Or do you insist that your thumbprint sink in—heralding decay wherever you press! I am helpless. (*Singing*)

I cannot ask you

To love my daughter.

She is to be pitied.

Do not bruise the fruit.

Do not bruise the fruit.

Do not bruise the fruit

That my wife bore and I planted.

Let it lie.
Let it lie.
Let it lie.

CHARLES (*Stuttering*)   L-l-l-l-let me g-g-g-go.
(SISTER THALIA *enters. She pulls* MR. VERDUN *away from* CHARLES *and leads* CHARLES *to the piano.* VIVIENNE, MR. VERDUN, *and* SISTER THALIA *exit*)

CHARLES (*Singing*)
Charles Anduit is my name,
And I do it all the same.
Stutter while I seek out fame.
Repetition is my game.
Take a straight and simple word
Of one syllable you've heard.
If I say it you'll regret
You can't catch it with a net.
(VIVIENNE *sticks her head out of the curtain*)

VIVIENNE   Say a simple word like love.

CHARLES (*Stuttering*)   L-l-l-l-l-ove. (*Singing*)
Charles Anduit is my name,
And I do it all the same.
Stutter while I seek out fame,
Stutter while I seek out,
Stutter while I seek
Stutter while I
Stutter while
Stutter
Stutt.
(*He exits*)

MR. VERDUN (*Entering with* VIVIENNE)   Well, he's gone, and good riddance to bad rubbish.
(*The curtain opens, revealing* MRS. VERDUN *and* PETER *arm in arm*)

PETER Don't we make a charming couple!

MR. VERDUN Ask me no questions, I'll tell you no lies.

PETER Such character! You look exhausted though. Why don't you sit down, and you too, my dear— (*To* MRS. VERDUN) You need the muse. I've written a poem.

MR. VERDUN Go ahead, abuse the muse.
(*They seat themselves on the couch.* PETER *stands.* FATHER SHENANAGAN *and* SISTER THALIA *are rapt with anticipation and beam toward* PETER *with hands in prayerful attitude*)

PETER I'll begin at the beginning and end at the end. (*He recites*)
Pussy cat, pussy cat where have you been?
I've been to London to visit the Queen.
Pussy cat, pussy cat, what did you there?
I lapped up a virgin without any hair.

MR. VERDUN At least it was short. Did you just make it up? I mean, did it just come to you? A sudden inspiration? What mervelous thing are you to have done it?

PETER I am an amateur and my purpose is love. Vivienne is an amateur also.

MRS. VERDUN Aren't we all!

MR. VERDUN Father Shenanagan and Sister Thalia are professionals, dear wife.

SISTER THALIA Only in the sense that we are sustained, um, arrive at staple means, um, do what we are cut out for without actually starving. It's a calling and we are answering.

MR. VERDUN I hear nothing. It's a soundproof existence.

SISTER THALIA You haven't been called.

MRS. VERDUN He wants to respond but hates crowds.

PETER   My advice is never rush into anything.

FATHER SHENANAGAN   We really must be going. All's well that ends well.

PETER   How you've summed it up, Father Shenanagan! I must go too and leave that delightfully mean man with his equally delightful wife. (*He goes up to* MR. VERDUN) I hope you're not insulted. I've had a simply gorgeous time!
> (*He exits with a flourish. The curtain closes.* SISTER THALIA *appears in front of the curtain*)

SISTER THALIA (*Singing*)
> We must hurry;
> They are waiting for us at the seminary.

FATHER SHENANAGAN (*If possible,* FATHER SHENANAGAN *accompanies them with an accordian. He sings*)
> With wine?

SISTER THALIA
> Indeed, wine is seminal at the seminary.

FATHER SHENANAGAN
> You need never remove your headdress for me again.

SISTER THALIA
> But why? Have I failed you?

FATHER SHENANAGAN
> I am not sure I can control the results
> Resulting from an irreligious glimpse.
> I'm not a saint, you know.

BOTH
> (He's)
> (I'm) not a saint, you know,
> A saint, you know,
> A saint, you know.

SISTER THALIA
> You begged me. You wanted it.
> I didn't get to my knees by myself.

FATHER SHENANAGAN
> If you had no intention,
> Why did you come prepared?
> Why did you spread the rumor
> All over the cells?

BOTH
> In the dormitories,
> In the retreats,
> In the parsonage
> And the vicarage,
> And also at the rear left chapel

FATHER SHENANAGAN
> All the way back at Saint Patrick's Cathedral?

BOTH
> Why?

SISTER THALIA
> I was asked by Mother Superior
> To publish an explanatory tract.
> I had to go into details.

BOTH
> (My)
> (Your) mortification would not have been complete
> Without the details.
> The Mother Superior is playing on the same team,
> Is playing on the same team,
> Is playing on the same team.
>   (*The curtain opens*)

VIVIENNE   Where did Charles go?

MR. VERDUN   Out into the world, step by step.

VIVIENNE Say, maybe he stopped on the corner for a chocolate egg cream. I'm thirsty myself. Want a goody, Dad? I'm going out.

MR. VERDUN Yes, I think so—I'd like a box of nonpareils, salted pumpkin seeds, a licorice whip, chocolate money, malt balls, and an all-day sucker.

VIVIENNE Anything for you, Mom?

MRS. VERDUN Thank you darling—I'd like two slices of watermelon candy, five bulls-eyes, a Sugar Daddy, and a package of candy cigarettes.

VIOLET Miss Vivienne, girl, maybe you bring me back a lil somethin' too. I'd prefer to fust choice candy bananas, bubble gum, toasted coconut marshmallows, and a package of Black Jack gum.

VIVIENNE Bien entendu! Back in a juffy. Then we can have a real grab bag. Violet, you go make some lemonade.
(*They exit, making a lot of noise*)

MRS. VERDUN I worry when she gets like that: starts to talk French and offers to do favors. She's a nervous child, anything could happen. Poor child, she hasn't been the same since she bit into a frozen Milky Way. (*To* FATHER SHENANAGAN *and* SISTER THALIA) Could you kind of keep an eye on her when you go down? See that she doesn't talk to strangers.

SISTER THALIA Of course, of course.
(SISTER THALIA *and* FATHER SHENANAGAN *exit*)

MR. VERDUN Well, there they go. (*He closes the curtain*) Yes, there they all go, my dear wifey. Now we are alone again for the second time this evening, except for Violet, who will go to her tiny windowless room off the kitchen in a moment.

MRS. VERDUN (*Calling in to* VIOLET) Violet, are you making the lemonade? Make it snappy, please, Mr. Verdun is thirsty.

VIOLET (*Appearing from the kitchen*) It on the table awready. I g'wine lie down an rest ma weary bones till de candy come.
(VIOLET *sings "I'm g'wine" etc. backstage*)

MRS. VERDUN Violet is a handsome girl. Don't you agree?

MR. VERDUN You said it, kid!
(*The bed slides under the curtain, to the apron, and they sit on it*)

MRS. VERDUN I didn't expect such passionate articulation!

MR. VERDUN Forget it, baby, I'm still crazy about you.

MRS. VERDUN Kiss me. (*They kiss*) At times I want you out, but now I want you in. Come. "Andiam, andiam mio bene."
(MR. VERDUN *and* MRS. VERDUN *assume the wrestling hook-up position. They then wrestle, alternating advantage, and end with a cross-body pin and arm lock.* MR. VERDUN *tickles* MRS. VERDUN, *which renders her helpless. He pins her and wins the fall*)

MRS. VERDUN (*Disappointed, wanting more*) Two falls to a finish.

MR. VERDUN Okay, anything you say.

MRS. VERDUN Who's the referee?

MR. VERDUN Violet.

MRS. VERDUN In the dark?
(VIOLET *returns*)

VIOLET Am I bein' paged?

MRS. VERDUN Want to play a game?

VIOLET Lawda mercy, it don make no no-how to me.

MRS. VERDUN   Well, then, winner take all!

MR. VERDUN   No cheating.

VIOLET   I'll see to that.

MRS. VERDUN   Let's begin.
  (MR. VERDUN *and* MRS. VERDUN *resume the hook-up position on the bed.* VIOLET *remains to the right of the bed. The cast enters, each as he sings his own line*)

FATHER SHENANAGAN

  Let no man now diminish
  What takes two falls to a finish.

MRS. VERDUN

  If wrestling once will get it twice.

VIOLET

  Wouldn't three times make it nice?

ALL

  Let no man now diminish
  What takes two falls to a finish.

MR. VERDUN

  Though your muscles may be quivering,

JOHN

  Still, tis fate the blow delivering.

ALL

  Let no man now diminish
  What takes two falls to a finish.

PETER

  Once I slipped out of a hold,

VIVIENNE

  You are young, but the world is old.

ALL
> Let no man now diminish
> What takes two falls to a finish.

SISTER THALIA
> I have tried to break the habit
> > (*She tries to rip her habit open*)

CHARLES (*Stuttering*)
> More than wa-wa-wa-wa-wa-wa-wa-wa-once.

ALL (*quietly*)
> Let no man now diminish
> What takes two falls to a finish.
> > (*There is a pause. Then they all sing loudly*)
> Let no man now diminish
> What takes two falls to a finish.
> > (*There is a blackout*)

Curtain

(*The curtain opens for a reprise. The actors exchange roles. and sing choice bits to each other*)

The Investigation

CAST

JOE	A policeman.
SLOVAK	A detective.
LARRY VAIL	The teen-age suspect.
CHERRY COKE	The victim's teen-age sister.
HAROLD	Cherry's boy friend.

This play is to be played as burlesque: no visual gag too low; broad, clearly etched gestures. The set is simple and "pop"; the costumes likewise.

THE INVESTIGATION *was first presented by the Theatre Company of Boston in February, 1966, under the direction of Paul Benedict, with the following cast:*

(In order of appearance)

SLOVAK	Jerome Raphel
LARRY VAIL	Joseph Hindy
JOE	Paul Harrington
CHERRY COKE	Susan Channing
HAROLD	Richard Allen

It was subsequently presented by the New Dramatists' Committee in June, 1966, under the direction of Sherman Drexler, and by the Milwaukee Repertory Theater in October, 1966, under the direction of Thomas Bissinger.

SCENE 1

A room in the police station. LARRY VAIL *is in the "cage."* JOE *is at a desk. A typewriter with a questionnaire form in it is on the desk.* SLOVAK *is between desk and "cage."*

SLOVAK   You say your name is Larry Vail. V-a-i-l, yes?

LARRY   Yes, sir.

SLOVAK   I believe you.

LARRY   Yes, sir.

SLOVAK (*Swinging around very fast*)   You knew this girl?

LARRY   What girl, sir?

SLOVAK   The cute number who became a back number and then a morgue number. Correct?

LARRY   Lots of things happened.

SLOVAK   Answer yes or no.

LARRY   Yes. She was a classmate of mine.

SLOVAK   You knew her. (*Slowly*) You knew her.

LARRY   Everyone in class did.

SLOVAK   Ehem, what was that? Everyone? (*His voice rises*) Everyone? The girl is dead, Vail, and you insult her character!

LARRY   I mean whoever knew her, we said hello, unless we didn't feel like it. Sometimes I used to get low. You know.

SLOVAK   Know? Who knows? I don't know, I really don't. Tell me what got you low, Larry. Something you did to Merry?

LARRY   I didn't do nothing to her. I said hello. Everybody said hello. It would've been funny if we didn't say hello.

SLOVAK   Funny. (*He mulls it over*) Funny. You don't like to be laughed at, do you Larry? I sympathize with you, boy. I know how you feel. Ever want to take it out on those others—the ones who laughed? Even now I feel like beating the shit out of certain lying bastards! Tell me. I can help you. What got your goat? What'd they laugh at?

LARRY   Nothin'. They didn't laugh at me. They laughed at jokes.

SLOVAK   Sure you weren't the joke? The fall guy? The brunt of the joke? The dumb jerk who couldn't answer back?

LARRY   No, no, that isn't so. I'll tell you the joke. It was pretty funny, only maybe I shouldn't, this being a police station and all.

SLOVAK   Tell me that joke, Larry. Everything depends on it. I like to laugh (*Ominously*) I can laugh as well as the next one.

LARRY   Well, it's kind of a dirty joke.

SLOVAK   Man to man, kid!

LARRY   Maybe it isn't so funny.

SLOVAK   Let me be the judge of that.

LARRY   Damn it!

SLOVAK   What's buggin' you, kid?

LARRY   I forgot the punch line.

SLOVAK   Let it go for now. It'll come back to you. I can wait. Now, you live at . . .?

LARRY   Ten twenty-one East River Drive.

SLOVAK   Get that Joe? Ten twenty-one East River Drive.
(JOE *nods and types*)

LARRY   I'm seventeen, sir.

SLOVAK   Now who asked you to volunteer that information? Don't anticipate. I never anticipate and I get pleasantly surprised. For instance, I didn't know you. I have never anticipated knowing you, and yet, here you are pleasantly. Like it here, Vail?

LARRY   It's okay.

SLOVAK   Better than running with the dogs at night, huh?

LARRY   Who did that?

SLOVAK   Oh, I thought you were hiding out. We were looking for you, Larry. Didn't you know? High and low for you.

LARRY   Yes, sir.

SLOVAK   Yes what?

LARRY   Sir. Yes, sir.

SLOVAK   I'm not a sir, Vail. I'm a police officer. I protect the peace, and I suspect you have disturbed it in a very brutal way. Am I right?

LARRY   About what, officer?

SLOVAK   Am I right that you are a lousy felonious hard-up mother-fucking rapist! (*There is a pause*—SLOVAK *whispers*) of a very beautiful young corpse called Merry Coke. Merry Coke, a girl who had hoped to grow up into proud American motherhood and who . . . and who was sucked into hideous fear and death by someone. I say someone who just couldn't wait. Couldn't wait to get married. I hope I haven't startled you, Vail. Here's a Kleenex.

LARRY   I need a lawyer.

SLOVAK   The court will appoint one.

LARRY   I know my rights.

SLOVAK   Do you? Do you really, you son of a bitch? Good parochial schoolboy, eh? What'd you do, give up masturbating for bigger things?

LARRY   Don't talk that way, officer. It . . . it isn't right for you to talk that way in your uniform and all.

SLOVAK   You honor my uniform? Probably wanted to be a policeman when you were four years old. I can't say I blame you. It's a good life. (*He takes his gun out of the holster and examines the barrel, etc.*) Especially when you chance to meet up with a sex maniac. You can't tell a sex maniac by the way he looks. You can only tell him by his act. His act of desecration. His act that destroys not only his victim, but those who loved her and who will never recover. (*In a confidential tone*) You do sympathize with Merry's mother?

LARRY   Her mother?

SLOVACK   M-o-t-h-e-r! We all had one once, at the crucial time. Have you ever thought how mothers got to be mothers?

LARRY   No.

SLOVAK   Never thought of (*He spells it out*) M-o-t-h-e-r doing it?

LARRY   No. No, never! (*He screams*) I never think of her at all.

SLOVAK   Okay. I believe you, boy. Just teasing a little. But getting back to Merry's mother. Why do you think she named her Merry?

I'll tell you why. Because she was a merry creature. Happy, good natured, wouldn't hurt a fly, glad to be alive. Are you glad to be alive?

LARRY   Yes and no.

SLOVAK   If I was in your position, I'd wish I was dead. As dead as Merry.

LARRY   I do, I wish I was dead.

SLOVAK   But you'll have to hang on for a while . . . (*There is a pause*) process of law.

LARRY   I want to die.

SLOVAK   It isn't that bad, Larry. You're young, you may get off easy. You may squirm off the hook yet. But if you do, there'll be a hole this big in you.
   (*He gestures*)

LARRY   I . . . I hope not. I didn't do it anyway. I didn't.

SLOVAK   Then who did? Do you know? Who was screwing that piece of ass before he screwed it out of existence?

LARRY   I didn't know about her ass.

SLOVAK   What? What was that? You didn't know about her what?

LARRY   Her ass? I've never said that before. I only saw her in the uniform.

SLOVAK   Didn't it stick out? Didn't it make a kind of twin mountain at the bottom rear?

LARRY   I usually saw her sitting down. She wore a pleated skirt.

SLOVAK   A pleated skirt. Innocent fashion. Innocent enough, don't you agree?

LARRY Yes.

SLOVAK But when she walked and wiggled, walked and joggled, bent down, perhaps to pick up a dropped notebook? Perhaps then the fashion wasn't so innocent. Perhaps it was even provocative! Provocative enough to incite one Larry Vail into acts previously shoved under the pillow with a sticky handkerchief.

LARRY I respected her. I thought of her body as holy, as another womb for Jesus. I never did her any harm. I never meant her harm. She was my ideal.

SLOVAK More's the pity. More's the pity! I pity you more for your lost ideals. Young men should have ideals. I've seen her picture. She would have been any man's ideal. Well-stacked, huh? Don't you agree? A real milk wagon. Tits! Tits red as beets, brown way down, you know where.

LARRY STOP! That has nothing to do with me. She's dead, isn't she? She's dead and I didn't do it.

SLOVAK You did! (*He shouts*) You did do it, Larry Vail, and your life isn't worth a red cent. Think, and I don't have to think too hard. I've just come from the morgue. Think about that white belly, slit as if someone had to find something in a hurry and didn't have time to open it the right way. Want to know what we found?

LARRY Christ!

SLOVAK Almost! A male fetus just a few months short of the ascension. How can he ever rise again, when you've sinned enough to make him descend. You are making Christ descend lower, much lower than he had ever intended. Know how long a trip like that takes? Forever! And neither you nor I will be here to greet him. Confess, I beg you. Confess for your soul. (*He sobs, entreats*) What is your life in the wide weird void of eternity? But a confession can help you pass the time of day, if that's what's left, in calm contemplation. Please, please, Larry, do it.

LARRY   I can't.
(*He slumps down in the cage*)

SLOVAK   How'd ya like me to send for your dad?

LARRY   Christ!

SLOVAK   Enough of that profanity. Save it for your secret thoughts.
(LARRY *bangs his head against the bars of the cage*) Don't do
that, Larry, you'll hurt yourself.

LARRY   When can I go home?

SLOVAK   Home? Your home? I've heard about that from your
neighbors. Tell me, does your dad beat your mom? I mean hard,
throw her against the wall and then punch her in the belly, like
this? (*He demonstrates*) Work her over good, like this? (*He
demonstrates*) Maybe remodels her face. (LARRY *runs around
the cage like a trapped rat*) Easy there. Easy boy. She comes
through, doesn't she? Puts a little make-up on the next day,
combs her hair pretty, wears a starched housedress, heats up the
coffee. Soul of respectability, isn't she? Isn't she? She even goes
out in the hall to mop up the piss he muddled around in the
night before. She's clean and good, isn't she? Isn't she? And she
loves you and hates him, doesn't she? Doesn't she? And don't
you despise him and love her? Don't you? Don't you? All the
time listening to the giant steel ball knocking down the walls, the
walls of your home. Listening to him destroying, destroying the
shelter, shattering the night with his heavy home-made fist.
(*Pause*) And you've felt that fist too, haven't you?

LARRY   (*He lies down on the floor of the cage and looks up at the
ceiling*) I have. I have felt it, but I was between them. They
expected me to be there.

SLOVAK   And this girl Merry Coke. She was nice to you. Let you
. . . (*Very loud*) feel her up! Let you touch those woolen titties
till you went out of your mind with desire. And then you became a raving maniac, like your father. Just like your father, a

madman; mean, vicious, brutal. Only you didn't stop! No, you didn't stop. Because unlike your dad, you had no common bed to quiet down in. No warm back to throw your leg over, no night smell to call your own. You had you! And what were you? A small guilty kid. Small! A kid with a prick as hard as this stick ... (*He bangs his nightstick against the floor*) and nothing to bang. Then bing bang boom, the explosion! The struggle; the assault from which one came back. One bastard came back. Sure it was hello and goodbye for her. Hello, nice to see you. Goodbye, go to hell! Goodbye all right!

LARRY   I hardly knew her.

SLOVAK   But you got acquainted.

LARRY   I'm thirsty.

SLOVAK   Joe, some water for Larry Vail.
(JOE *gets a cup of water at the water cooler and gives it to* LARRY. LARRY *stands in the middle of the cage and slowly pours the water over his head*)

SLOVAK   The kid's nuts.
(*The phone rings.* JOE *answers*)

JOE   It's his mother.

SLOVAK   I'll talk to her. (SLOVAK *takes the phone*) Hello, Mrs. Vail, Detective Slovak here. I wonder if you could come talk to us at the station house? Oh, that's too bad. Well, then I think I can ask you a few questions on the phone. Now, Mrs. Vail, can you tell me what your son was doing the night of November 25, 1964 at eight P.M.? Can you tell me that? In bed,, I see, with a virus. Threw up. Never left the house? Sick as a dog and couldn't move. What if I told you I heard something different, something—oh, you don't believe me, m'am? Give me a chance. Why don't I give your son a chance? That's why I had you call me. I give everybody a chance. Just one moment, please. ... (*Turning to* LARRY) Have anything to say to your mom? She wants her soiled boy back. Wants to clean him up for the party. (LARRY *reaches for the phone through the bars of the cage. At first* SLOVAK *holds it just out of reach. Then he brings it over on a long extension wire*)

LARRY   Mom, mom? (*There is a pause*) There's no one there. The phone's dead.

SLOVAK   Everything you touch dies.
(LARRY *does a despairing kind of dance that ends with a catatonic pose*)

JOE (*To* SLOVAK)   He's very talented.

SLOVAK   Talented? The dance of death.

SCENE 2

A garage. There is a car sliced in half so that the audience can see into it. Hanging on the windshield is a small souvenir saint or Christ. The car has power steering and a wheel gear shift. It is up-holstered in real black leather. A teen-age girl (MERRY COKE's counterpart) walks onstage from the auditorium.

CHERRY   My name is Cherry Coke. I'm Merry's twin sister. It might have happened to me. Let me show you how. Come on out, Harold! (*She calls to the back of the garage*) Sometimes I call him Harry, or Hairy because he's so hairy. His hair goes all the way up his back and crawls out of his shirt cuffs and even his pants cuffs. I think that's very masculine, because girls aren't that way.

HAROLD   You said it! Girls are smooth. Smooth! Girls are cool. What say, Fox?

CHERRY   Let's pretend that I'm Merry and you're Larry.

HAROLD   Oh no.

CHERRY   Please?

HAROLD   No!

CHERRY   Why?

HAROLD   Rub it on your chest.

CHERRY   Afraid?

HAROLD   Okay, on one condition.

CHERRY   What?

HAROLD   You let me . . . you know what!

CHERRY   Maybe.

HAROLD   What're we waitin' for?
        (*Both exit and come right back in*)

HAROLD   So this is where your dad keeps his car.

CHERRY   Umm humm.

HAROLD   It's new.

CHERRY   Umm humm.

HAROLD   Say, can I get in and get the feel of the wheel?

CHERRY   Um humm.

HAROLD   You know, we don't have a car in our family.

CHERRY   Really? I can't remember when we didn't.

HAROLD   No, we never did, because of lots of reasons.

CHERRY   I guess there are reasons for everything.
        (*She snuggles up to him, pinning him against the body of*
        of the car)

HAROLD   Say, hey!

CHERRY   Silly!

HAROLD   Well, one of the reasons .

CHERRY   For what?

HAROLD   Why we didn't have a car.

CHERRY   Oh.

HAROLD   My dad's money was all tied up . . . in booze.

CHERRY   You shouldn't say such things about . . . secrets.

HAROLD   I know, but you're so nice.

CHERRY   Yes, I am. Want to go into the car?

HAROLD   Anything, yeah sure!

CHERRY   Just slide in. It's soft as a slipper.

HAROLD   (*He slides in behind the wheel*)   Whee! This gives me such a sense of . . . of power. I could do anything.

CHERRY   (*She slides in beside him*)   Anything?

HAROLD   Umm humm.

CHERRY   Try this on for size.
(*Gives him a cloying kiss*)

HAROLD   Christ! Do . . . do you? I mean, that was great. I think I don't know what to do. You're so great and all.

CHERRY   I'm not really that great. Napoleon was greater.

HAROLD (*Laughs*)   Napoleon was a screw.

CHERRY   So are you, little boy!
(*She musses his hair so that it looks like Napoleon's*)

HAROLD   I'm not little and you're a screw too. What would your mother say if she found you out here with me?

CHERRY   I don't know.

HAROLD   Don't you?

CHERRY   No.

HAROLD She'd call you a prostitute.
(*He has trouble pronouncing the word*)

CHERRY Really? Who asked you to share the wealth? I didn't force you in here. You're a dirty-minded pig.

HAROLD Easy! You're getting me mad.

CHERRY Easy, you're getting me mad! I'm mad too, and if you want to know about my mother, she isn't my mother. She's my step-mother. I step on her and she steps on me and that's why I'm dirty all over!

HAROLD What are you getting so mad for? I didn't mean it.

CHERRY Oh, you meant it all right. They all mean it. My step-mother means it too, like if she caught me with you right now, know what she'd say?

HAROLD No.

CHERRY She'd say, "Cherry, stop hustling in your daddy's new car. You'll destroy the upholstery."

HAROLD Stop it, Cherry, or is it Merry. You look just like your twin sister. How can I tell you apart?

CHERRY (*She opens her legs and pulls up her skirt*) Look, take a good long look.
(HAROLD *stares down at her legs*)

HAROLD I don't know what I'm supposed to see.

CHERRY I have a birthmark right on the inside of my thigh. She doesn't. It's a pretty color, isn't it?

HAROLD Your skirt must be over it. I can't see a thing.

CHERRY (*Looks down and laughs*) Oh yeah, you're really right.
(*She pulls her skirt higher*)

HAROLD   I see it now. It looks like a tiny heart. Is it flat or raised. I'd like to feel it. It looks like velvet.

CHERRY   Suit yourself.

HAROLD   Mean it?

CHERRY   Yeah, really.
(HAROLD *touches the spot and then suddenly darts down and kisses it*)

HAROLD   It's marvelous! It's just like a greeting card.

CHERRY   Yeah, and what does it say?

HAROLD   It says "Hearts are red, boys are blue . . ."

CHERRY   Yes, go on, what next?

HAROLD   What I'd like to do to you.

CHERRY   Is that a proper request.

HAROLD   I'm sincere, Cherry. I love you, you're the most!

CHERRY (*Preening*)   Really?

HAROLD   Yes, May I sample your charms?

CHERRY   Why not! Say, do you have a cigarette?

HAROLD   I don't smoke.

CHERRY   Oh well, you're a real clean livin' kid.

HAROLD   Does that bother you?

CHERRY   I don't know. Maybe you're too good for me.

HAROLD   Oh no! Oh no! You're too good for me.

CHERRY   Keep that in mind! Say, you are pretty sincere, aren't you? You really like me. I mean really. You won't tell on me, will you?

HAROLD   May God strike me dead.

CHERRY   Oh that's funny, asking Him to bother about you. You know, He's liable to.

HAROLD   He won't, because I keep my word.

CHERRY   Anyway, He might do it anyway if that's what He wants to do. He'd do it to anybody and He might even do it to me at any time too.

HAROLD   Please don't talk about Him.

CHERRY   Religious or somethin'?

HAROLD   Or somethin'.
(*She grabs him and they fall down on the car seat, him on top of her*)

CHERRY   Like me?

HAROLD   Ummmm.

CHERRY   Do you know how to do it?

HAROLD   Help me.

CHERRY   It's easy, like this. (*She guides him. The lights go out and back on in two seconds flat.* CHERRY *and* HAROLD *sitting side by side*) You're not much, are you? I say you're pretty small, aren't you? Did you come? Say something.

HAROLD   No. I mean I don't know. It was like wriggling through the mud and then someone threw a glass of water in my face.

CHERRY   Don't you like me any more?

139

HAROLD So that's what it's all about. I hate it. I hate it. It's nothing, and you made me do it. You're bad. You're bad and you made me bad. We've sinned. Do you realize that? I hate you. Oh boy, look at my uniform! My pants are all stained.

CHERRY So are mine, and my skirt.

HAROLD You're the worst stain. The worst in the world. I want to rub out the stain.

CHERRY Say, hey, don't look at me that way, as if you want to kill me.
(HAROLD *puts his hands around her neck and proceeds to choke her*)

HAROLD Prostitute! Prostitute! You won't tell about me. (*They struggle and finally she lays limp and dead.* HAROLD *taps her. She sits up abruptly*) Gee, do you think that's the way it happened?

CHERRY No. I don't think so. I got carried away, didn't you?

HAROLD I'm a born actor.

CHERRY This is very exciting, really. Are you terrific!

HAROLD I enjoy my work.

CHERRY Let's do it again soon!

HAROLD Right now?

CHERRY Uh uh. Dad has to use the car. Oh, poor Sis, she would have to be dead and miss all the fun. I was always the lucky one. Do you believe in luck? (HAROLD *accidently leans on the horn and it blows loudly. He jumps back in alarm. Then they both laugh*) That wasn't so lucky. Let's get out of here before they find us.
(*They rush out of the garage*)

Blackout

Back in the station house.

SLOVAK   Joe, you know what I'm gonna do for this boy?

JOE   Can't guess.

SLOVAK   I'm gonna entertain him. He entertained us, didn't he?

JOE   Yeah, he was very entertaining.

SLOVAK   We oughta keep him happy while his mother's gone.

JOE   I thought he was happy, Officer Slovak. I seen him dance.

SLOVAK   Now he's gonna see me dance, Joe. He's gonna see me
dance now, because he ain't never gonna go to no Policeman's
Ball to see this. This is kinda special. Only for shut-ins. Okay,
bring in the kid's uniform.
   (JOE *goes out and brings in* MERRY COKE's *school uniform.
   It is neatly hung on a hanger—pleated skirt and jumper
   top. It is ripped and stained*)

JOE   I'll hang it on the chair.
   (*He hangs it on the chair*)

SLOVAK   Now then. The lady is seated. Comfortable dear? You
look lovely tonight, except for a few unavoidable details. I'm
glad you came to the dance because there's no one in the whole
world I'd rather dance with than you. We have a mutual friend.
Remember Larry Vail? He recommended you to me. I could
hardly believe it, that he would want to get us together, because
I'm really much older than you. Of course that didn't bother
Errol Flynn, but I'm no Errol Flynn. Do you find me attractive?

Well, perhaps tolerable? Tolerable enough to trip the light fantastic with? (SLOVAK *lifts the uniform off the chair and starts to dance the waltz with it. He hums crazily as he dances*) Am I holding you too tight, baby? You like it that way? Say, I like it too. In fact, even though it's early in the dance, I'd like to reserve the next one. Oh, you'd love to? No, no, I'm the lucky one. You're so young, so sweet, so delightful to hold. Say listen, you understand, of course, that this is strictly between us. I mean, don't let it get out, because, you know, my wife is a little old fashioned. She's a good wife and mother but "Oh you kid!" Never danced the waltz before? We're even. I never danced the twist. Doesn't mean I won't. If you're willing to teach me, I'm willing to learn. I'll try anything once. Say, even though we both know Larry and like him, don't you think he's too quiet. Even a little strange? I mean, has he ever kissed you or anything like that? Anyone would. (*He kisses the air and then the uniform with loud smacks of his lips*) He hasn't? I wonder what's holding him back. How does he look at you? As if he wants to eat you up, but you think he left his teeth upstairs in the drawer? I'm sorry for him, aren't you? The way he's all bottled up. My luck, his misfortune. I can't help it if I'm so forward. I like to have a good time. You're like me, aren't you, Merry? Just raring to go!

JOE Terrific! I think the kid appreciates your efforts, Slovak. How about after the dance?

SLOVAK After the dance? Ah yes, but gentlemen don't speak about after the dance. Do they, Larry? (*He whirls around to snap his question at* LARRY. *He hangs the uniform on the cage*) Do they Larry? They don't tell about how it was! How suddenly Merry Coke's pulse jumped its pressure points and went hop-scotching it all the hell over her fragile pulsating body, until it got tired and just plain stopped dead. Gentlemen don't tell. But punks can be made to tell, can be made to garble the whole thing out in spite of themselves. Ever vomit, Larry? Mother stick her finger down your throat, like this! (*He grabs* LARRY *through the bars, lifts him to a standing position and jams his finger down* LARRY'S *throat.* LARRY *retches but does not actually throw up*) Hope I didn't make you sick. My hands are clean, and that's more than

I can say for you. (*He drops* LARRY) Let's have a moment's silence in memory of the deceased in whose honor we are all gathered here today. (SLOVAK *drops his head in mock respect.* LARRY *crawls over to just under the uniform. It is hanging low enough so that he can lean his cheek against the skirt. He fondles it*) So, Vail, you're a sentimental slob. Want it for a souvenir? Maybe you'd like to wear it to the trial? Make quite a stir. Oh, but that's not possible, you're too big. Much bigger. You're absolutely ungainly compared to Merry Coke. You're a gangling, grisly, giant of a boy. You couldn't even get your head through the top. When you choked Merry to death, Larry lad, was it as easy as crushing a box of Cracker Jacks, or did it have more the give of a half-ripe persimmon? Shaking your head, are you? Hasn't mother ever brought you a persimmon from the fruit store? An exotic fruit, I grant you, but available. I'll get you one if you confess. The juicier the confession, the riper the fruit. Is it a deal? I'd like to see both running out of your mouth at the same time. (*He yawns*) My, I'm getting tired. Will you excuse me for a moment. I have to refresh myself. (*He leaves the room.* JOE *puts his feet on the desk and goes to sleep.* LARRY *fondles the skirt. He talks to it. He mumbles to the skirt and moans to it, all unintelligible. He inhales the skirt and crushes it between his hands. He smooths it out and stares at it. He faints.* SLOVAK *re-enters*) Awfully quiet in here. The quiet is good. It breeds reverses. It revives intuition and renews the spirit. Get up, Larry. Your inquisitor is back. Get up, damn you, I have some more questions. (SLOVAK *goes over and examines* LARRY. *He realizes that he has fainted or had a stroke or something. He unlocks the cage and carries* LARRY *to a leather couch at the side of the room*) Oh Larry, Larry, get up!

> (SLOVAK *fans* LARRY's *head with his policeman's hat or one that he takes from a shelf.* LARRY *stirs. His hand flops to the floor. He groans*)

LARRY Where am I?

SLOVAK You're here with me, Larry.

LARRY Who are you?

SLOVAK   Your friend. I want to talk to you.

LARRY   Talk to me?

SLOVAK   Yes, I like you Larry, and seeing as how we're in the same boat together . . .

LARRY   Boat?

SLOVAK   Ship?

LARRY   Three smokestacks and three decks.

SLOVAK   I think we're on to something. Joe, take this down.

LARRY   Three decks: a lower, an upper and one in the middle. She walked from the lower to the upper and they examined her ticket.

SLOVAK   It wasn't tied to her toe by any chance?

LARRY   She took it out of her handbag and showed it to them. They, I mean he, didn't let her up. She said "I just want to see what it's like up here." And he said "Go back." So she went down a ladder and stopped in the middle. She sat down on a deck chair. She was in the middle and the middle got smaller and smaller. She screamed, but no one could help her. There was no one else there to stop the crusher.

SLOVAK   You were there, Larry.

LARRY   No, I wasn't.

SLOVAK   Then how do you know about it?

LARRY   I don't know.

SLOVAK   I know! You were the guy at the controls. Once you got your hand on that lever, the decks went. They went all the way until they were joined in the middle by a very tasty paste of blood, bones and guts. Did they have to pry your hand loose? Did you do it yourself after you came to? Do you think it was the cold steel of the lever that ran in your veins afterwards? Or was it fear? Fear that makes cowards or heros out of ordinary men? Are you a coward or a hero, Larry?

LARRY   It was just a dream.

SLOVAK   Coward? Or hero? What are you to yourself?

LARRY   I'm a coward, only not always. I don't want to be. But I don't like to get hurt.

SLOVAK   No, I know you don't. You'd rather deal it out. Hurt first, protect yourself. It's only natural. I don't blame you. Self-protection is a funny thing, Vail. It destroys everything in its path, and when that's done it turns back up the road and destroys itself. You don't get away with nasty acts, Larry, because sometimes there are witnesses. I say sometimes, because this is one of those times. You were observed, Larry Vail. Prepare to meet your accusers. Among them is your nemesis.

LARRY   I don't know what that means.

SLOVAK   Big words for big deeds. But somehow the deed gets done without the word.

LARRY   I don't know what that word means.
(LARRY *turns over on his belly on the couch and hides his head.* SLOVAK *caresses* LARRY'*s head and rubs his back*)

SLOVAK   Well, it's like this, son. You know, I've always wanted a son. I'm a sporting man, enjoy hunting, fishing, ball games, women. Never had a son to share those things with. Had three daughters. Queens, every one of them. Good to their mom and dad. Nothing left to be desired. Married well, ah, but I'm boring you, Larry. What I want to say is I've got no one, no son to call my own, till you. I'd like to teach you things, correct your spelling, check your sums, bring you maps to hang in your room. Geography, history, the whole works, even, even . . . (*He turns to* JOE) Say Joe, you got a Webster's handy? (JOE *hands him a pocket dictionary*) Let's do a little homework together, son. Let's see, nemesis. N-E-M-E-S-I-S, got it? It says here— (*He shakes* LARRY) Larry, you're not looking. If you don't pay attention I'll take back the car keys, boy. You don't deserve privileges unless you do your work. Now, the work at hand is word study. In the beginning was the word, and it's stayed with us ever since, I hope it will remain with you for at least long enough for you to get it through your thick skull that you're cornered, Larry Vail. And the word will prevail, will prevail! (LARRY *tears himself away from the unwanted caress and mental torture of* SLOVAK. *He rushes for the door as if to escape. He pounds on it and pulls on the handle. He tries to break it down with his shoulder. He ends up leaning against it and crying*) That shoulder business, Larry, that's movie stuff. I locked that sturdy door myself. You can't get out. Come back to me, and we'll continue the lesson. I have my finger in the place. We won't waste time.

LARRY Please don't talk any more. Just leave me alone.

SLOVAK I can't, Larry. I can't leave you alone. If I left you alone, Larry, there'd be one more unsolved crime in the annals of crime history. I think I have you. Now Officer Kroll here will help you to your proper seat beside me. Now! (JOE *helps* LARRY *back to the couch*) Now! It says here: Nemesis 1. the goddess of retribution or vengeance. 2. an agent of retribution or punishment. We have many such visitors in this station house yearly, Vail. Many goddesses and many agents. As you may know from your early mythology, they often appear in disguise, but it is not long before they reveal themselves to the party concerned and carry out a terrible punishment. The pointing finger is sharpened, Larry. Beware lest your wounds increase. Take him away, Joe. Put him back in the cage. I can't bear to look at his sick, sick face. (JOE *takes* LARRY *back to the cage more dead than alive. He sits on the floor and searches in his pockets for a comb. He finds it and begins to nervously comb his hair*) What that boy needs is some Wildroot Cream Oil, Joe. It'd make his day worthwhile.

(*Starts declaiming as an actor would*) We all seek for love. Some do it with a lamp that lights up the entire universe. Some do it with a tramp who shuts off the lights, won't let us see because she's about to pass something extra along. Healthy, Larry? Have you noticed, I mean have you noticed yet, what you got when you got her? Not only was Merry Coke pregnant when you terminated her existence, she was diseased. Funny, the deceased was diseased. Sure, I thought she was a good girl. But when I was out just before I got the lab report, and it was a shock. A distinct shock. Have trouble urinating? Any burning sensation? We'll have to get the doctor to examine you, Larry. Every little clue counts, and of course, you wouldn't want it to run its course. Those galloping gonococci may have you by the balls, kid! Wouldn't want to lose your bounce, would you?

LARRY   I don't believe it.

SLOVAK   What you believe doesn't matter, Larry. Unfortunately, what does matter is the facts, and I've got them. In a few minutes we're going on a trip, boy, to familiar hunting grounds. You're going to re-enact the crime for us.

LARRY   I'm not the one you're looking for.
    (*He nervously bites his knuckles*)

SLOVAK   (*Disgusted, he shakes his head and clucks his tongue*) Yeah, yeah, come on. Let's go!
    (*He starts to unlock the cage. The lights dim*)

Curtain

The garage, exactly as before. The little Christ statue is still hanging on the windshield; it is somewhat obvious, perhaps fluorescent, so that when the lights go out it dominates. Superimpose a colored slide projected behind it on the wall so that the statue is larger than life. SLOVAK, LARRY *and* JOE *are standing around.*

SLOVAK   Move around. Don't be afraid. See if you like the place, Larry. It's just a garage, and that's just a car. Comfortable too. (*He jumps in the car and bounces up and down on the cushions*) Care to join me?

LARRY   I can see from here.

SLOVAK   What do you see?

LARRY   A car in a garage. I know whose garage, too.

SLOVAK   I know you do, Larry. There's no trick involved here. I wasn't going to take you into any old garage. Our time is too valuable for that. Get in!

LARRY   Must I?

SLOVAK   Yes. You must! Here, I'll get out and you get in. Get all the way in, right behind the wheel!
    (JOE *shoves him into the car and* LARRY *sits there like a corpse*)

LARRY   Now what?

SLOVAK   Pretend you're a studious, well-mannered boy waiting for a date. Fidget around, straighten your tie, do the comb bit!

Finger your fly, make sure it's up. Go ahead, do what I tell you.
You enjoy a good reputation around here, Vail, don't you?

LARRY   I guess so.

SLOVAK   Some of your friends told me you wanted to be a mission-
ary. Was that before or after the crime?

LARRY   What crime?

SLOVAK   The Merry Coke crime!

LARRY   I always wanted to serve the church.

SLOVAK   Let us hope you serve it as an example!

LARRY   Yes, sir.

SLOVAK   Now, you are a well-bred, repressed fink, waiting for his
date. On the outside nothing out of the ordinary, but on the inside, turbulent crap grappling in the mudpit of your very being!
I understand these things, Larry. I was a Bible reader in my
youth. I'm a believer, but I too have had bad thoughts. Yes, and
have even strayed miserably. Got lost once too.

LARRY   Yes, sir.

SLOVAK   There's that sir again! We're not in England, Vail, and
I'm not the headmaster. Cut it out! Now, where was I, Joe?

JOE   You were setting him up for his date.

SLOVAK   Right! Larry, you are now imagining those soft, lacy
things women wear. You've seen them on clotheslines all over the
neighborhood. You've seen them on TV and in the newsreels.
They hang everywhere, shamelessly! But they hang most shamelessly in your own mind, blotting everything else out!
     (LARRY's *hands tremble on the wheel. He pulls out a
     Kleenex to wipe his forehead. He crumples it up and tosses
     it on the floor*)

149

LARRY Are you speaking to me, Officer Slovak?

SLOVAK To you, at you, for you. Got anything to say? Want to add anything of your own, first hand?

LARRY No.

SLOVAK Not yet? You will. You'll want to. You'll turn yourself inside out to tell. You'll tell all and then, then, you'll rest.

JOE Ready yet, Slovak?

SLOVAK Soon, soon, Joe. We mustn't tip our mitt before he's prepared. Larry, say Larry, would you mind picking up that Kleenex you threw on the floor of the car. It isn't our car and we don't want to offend the owners with untidy habits. Remember the last toss-away you left in the car? (LARRY *shakes his head and grips the wheel, pressing his back against the seat*) You should remember. It was the corpse of Merry Coke! I don't say you didn't try to remove her, but you panicked! And in your panic you left a mighty mess for Homicide to clean up. We did a thorough job. Finished the floor and fittings with a portable vacuum cleaner. Then we took it back to the "lab" and sifted the whole thing out.

JOE Dandruff, hair, sand, and dried blood, bobby pins, button, potato chip, nail off of a finger, and a scrap of paper.

SLOVAK You've memorized it.

JOE Yeah.

SLOVAK Fine, fine, now keep alert. Larry here doesn't like lists. They bore him. This list in particular. Now, if the A and P didn't stock all these items, where in heaven's name could I get them? Oh, I know. Go to the source! That's it. Eliminate the middleman. Larry, Larry, I'm talking to you! A lesson in economics never hurt anybody. Or do you think you know too much? Listening? (LARRY *nods his head*) As I was saying: luckily, Larry had no middleman to deal with, unless you consider his conscience. He could go direct to the source, and what a rich source! Gay, pretty, giggling, carefree Merry Coke. She was giving samples that evening. But she didn't have to advertise. Larry here said "I'll buy!" And he wrapped her up with her own shiny white belt and subdued the still-struggling Merry Coke whose face was now a mask of panic! (*He darts toward* LARRY *as if to attack him*) Was that so? You know you did it. Did you notice? Mask of panic. Panic swept over her. Then, he, you, Larry, that's where we have you! then he stuffed her mouth with Kleenex. She shut up. Her eyes were still open though. Remember her eyes, Larry? Close yours and recollect. Her eyes, your hands, your claws ripping her thin undergarments into remnants. The package was tied too tightly, Larry. She stopped struggling. Didn't move at all. Then it was time for butchery. Larry, you bastard, the knife wasn't even yours. God, I can't hardly stand it. (*He turns to* JOE) Can you stand it, Joe?

JOE   No, I can't hardly stand it. Emotion is choking me.

SLOVAK   Emotion is choking us, why isn't it choking him? (*He darts toward* LARRY *again*) Let's feel your hands, Larry. His palms are sweaty, Joe. He's coming along. He's coming along so good we can take it nice and easy with him. Relax, Larry. You are once again waiting; she comes through the garage door, she sneaks in. It's a secret meeting.

LARRY   Why are you doing this to me?

SLOVAK   You know why, Larry. We want to help you unburden yourself. We also have a *public* to please. They're very interested in the case. *You* may not want to relive the past, you may even believe it never happened, but they don't want you to tell a lie. They want you to say: yes! Come on boy, spit it out!

JOE   (*Doing a Fred Astaire act*)   He won't sing, can't make him, he won't sing, can't make him, he won't sing 'cause he won't sing.

SLOVAK   He won't sing because he's choking on the words

LARRY No.

SLOVAK When you go to hell, mister, the ladies are gonna ram
their hot little pants down your throat and you're gonna have to
take it. Sweating again? Here, use my handkerchief.
(*He pulls a pair of white panties out of his breast pocket
and throws them into* LARRY's *face. He then turns around in
mock disgust*)

JOE Maybe he doesn't know what note to start on. He'd like to
sing, but—

SLOVAK (*Turning sharply to* LARRY *again*) Larry, what's your key?
Let's hear a note. (SLOVAK *sings a very low note*) Is that it? Too
low? Maybe a little higher. Try this. (SLOVAK *sings a few notes
in fag falsetto*) Too high? (*He reaches into his pocket and pulls
out a piece of paper with something written on it*) I have written
the words down very carefully for you, Larry. These are the
words to the song; words we don't want to forget. Here, take it. I
want you to know that I have the soul of a poet. Joe, bring me
my attaché case.
(JOE *goes out to get the attaché case*)

LARRY I'm too nervous; I can't read.

SLOVAK Even seasoned performers are nervous before a debut, Mr.
Vail. Let me give you an idea of what I want, but it's up to you
to do something creative with it. (SLOVAK *takes the paper back
and reads from it in an expressionless way, as if reading aloud
to his wife about a sale on couches*)
I, Larry Vail, do hereby confess
To murdering Merry in her little dress.
To strangling and raping and making a mess,
To all of these charges the answer is yes.
I, Larry Vail, the powers invoke
To snuff out my life as I did Merry Coke,
To shave me, unbelt me, and lead me to croak.
I'm guilty, I know it, for death is no joke.
(JOE *comes back in with the attaché case*)

JOE Here's the magic kit.
   (*Pats it affectionately*)

SLOVAK Hold on to it. Look at that kid; one of the coolest ice cubes
   I've ever come across.

JOE Shows no emotion. You're questioning a vegetable.

SLOVAK What that vegetable needs is a pile of shit shoveled on it.

JOE What's that you're holding?

SLOVAK It's a song I wrote for Larry. He's about to adapt it to his
   own style. Here, take it! (SLOVAK *shoves the confession at* LARRY,
   who takes it) Sorry I left my pitch pipe at home, but sing to me
   anyway (*Suddenly whipping his gun out and threatening* LARRY
   with it) or I'll play the scale right up and down your cracked
   keyboard!

JOE We can say he tried to get away.

LARRY I, Larry Vail—
   (*He hesitates*)

SLOVAK Climb up on the car, Vail; so we can observe you from a
   vantage point.
      (LARRY *climbs on top of the car.* SLOVAK *and* JOE *sit on the
      floor crosslegged, chin in the palm of both hands, looking up
      admiringly, like kids around a campfire*)

LARRY (*Sings in a counter-tenor; actually angelic, choirboy voice*)
   I, Larry Vail, do hereby confess
   To murdering Merry in her little dress,
   To strangling and raping and making a mess,
   To all of these charges the answer is yes.
   I, Larry Vail, the powers invoke
   To snuff out my life as I did Merry Coke,
   To shave me, unbelt me, and lead me to croak,
   I'm guilty, I know it, for death is no joke.
      (*Both men help* LARRY *down*)

SLOVAK You not only dance well, you sing like a bird. I have something to add. (*He punches* LARRY *in the gut*) The punch line!

JOE It's a pleasure to work with you. Never a dull moment.

SLOVAK It takes time and care to polish an act, Joe. You've seen me come up from the ranks. I wouldn't even say I need inspiration any more. No, inspiration is for amateurs—I work cool; I calculate my effects; I practice with the materials at hand; sometimes I improvise, but I never lose an audience. (LARRY *tries to get up.* SLOVAK *points to* LARRY) My material is reassembling itself. Joe, open the kit. (JOE *opens the attaché case. In it are toys, puzzles, noisemakers, and a rubber hose.* JOE *hands the hose to* SLOVAK) Now he's gonna put his John Hancock right on the line. I won't take any excuses.
   (*He threatens* LARRY *with the hose. He shoves the paper under* LARRY's *nose and gives him a pen. Then he starts to guide* LARRY's *hand like a teacher, but decides to let* LARRY *do it alone. As* LARRY *writes, he says*)

LARRY What will people think of me now?

SLOVAK (*Disgustedly*) What did they ever think of you?
   (LARRY *hands the confession to* SLOVAK. SLOVAK *embraces him with one arm around the shoulder, sort of "all is forgiven." In the other hand he holds the confession.* JOE *walks over and takes the confession out of* SLOVAK's *hand. As he looks at the confession he becomes incredulous*)

JOE Say, Slovak, he signed your name to it. Look!
   (SLOVAK *takes the paper slowly. He stares at it in disbelief. Meanwhile* LARRY *has sneaked behind* SLOVAK *and pulled his gun out of the holster*)

LARRY Stand back against the wall. I don't want to hurt you.

JOE Throw the gun down, Larry.

LARRY I don't throw anything away.

SLOVAK   Use that revolver and you're finished.

LARRY   I don't have anything to lose.

JOE   Larry, you have a chance, don't let Slovak fool you. It's his job to get tough. He likes you.

LARRY   I don't know. Maybe I'll finish his job for him.

SLOVAK   You've got the gun but you don't have the "heart."

JOE   Don't egg him on, Slovak, he means it.

SLOVAK   Tell us, Larry, did you or didn't you? I wouldn't want my conscience to bother me.

LARRY   (*Pointing to parts of his body, his eyes, nose, mouth, ears, chest, stomach, genitals;* LARRY *recites in the manner of "He loves me, he loves me not"*)   I did it, I did it not, I did it, I did it not, I— (*He rubs his eyes*) My eyes hurt.

SLOVAK   Larry, listen to me.

LARRY   I'd rather you didn't say things to me. I want it very quiet now. I want it quiet so that I can go away.
  (*Softly and stiffly* LARRY *backs away, then he whirls around and shoots himself in the stomach. He doubles over.* SLOVAK *and* JOE *rush over to* LARRY)

SLOVAK   Get an ambulance, Joe.

JOE   The poor jerk was out of his mind.

SLOVAK   Yeah, out of his, into mine. (*JOE goes out to radio the call for an ambulance.* SLOVAK *squats down next to the dead* LARRY, *picks up one of his limp hands and leans his cheek against it. Then he whispers with emotion*) Larry . . .
  (*The lights dim on the tableau. There is the sound of sirens*)

Curtain

Hot Buttered Roll

CAST

JAN   A call girl.

JORDAN   A purveyor of burly girls.

SAVAGE   A weak old man, also a billionaire.

JEWEL   A female bodyguard.

HOT BUTTERED ROLL *was first presented in June, 1966, by the New Dramatists' Committee under the direction of Melvin Bernhardt. It was subsequently presented by the Milwaukee Repertory Theater in October, 1966, under the direction of Thomas Bissinger, with the following cast:*

(In order of appearance)

CORRUPT SAVAGE	Thomas Tarpey
JEWEL	Rhoda B. Carrol
JAN	Rebecca Lombard
JORDAN	Michael Fairman

The scene opens in the bedroom of MR. CORRUPT SAVAGE. *He is
in bed reclining against three huge pillows. His hair is a gray bush
resembling Colette's. He is wearing tinted eyeglasses. Strewn over
his bed and on his pillow and in his lap are girlie magazines. He is
perusing one intently and reads out loud.*

SAVAGE   Irish McCalla, incredible yardage. Yas, that gal is pretty
fat linoleum. Money-back guarantee, wal, I don't expect to not
like! I expect to keep my big glossies, 39½, 25, 36, Irish dear—
(*He kisses the magazine*) turn you upside down and do your
eggs for you. (*He calls loudly*) Jewel, my eggs! Nasty monster,
that woman, even a whale can play possum. (*He calls again*)
Jewel, I'm sloshing around again!
    (JEWEL *kicks the door open since she is carrying a tray.
    On it is an open can of beans, two soft-boiled eggs, buttered
    toast, coffee, and one perfect rose.* JEWEL *is a huge, robust
    woman. She is obviously in charge*)

JEWEL   Stop thrashing about, you'll tire yourself out. (*She lays
the tray on a bed table at the foot of the bed, and rolls it up to
SAVAGE's lap*) What're you lookin' at now?

SAVAGE   Her sensuous charms are available to me. Look, she's
much too hot to be warm.

JEWEL   Men! Men! Men! You'd think I wasn't enough woman
for any man.

SAVAGE   Want quick action? Butter my toast and crack my eggs,
this offer will not be repeated.

JEWEL   You don't intend to eat first?

SAVAGE   First from what?

JEWEL The sheets, Corrupt, they must be changed. Jan is coming to see you right after you eat.

SAVAGE It's your fault you put the tray right under my nose.

JEWEL I forgot, but I can't make thousands happy, the way your ladies do.

SAVAGE I hired you through the private mailways, and I believed Big Ten-in-One was complete for one dollar.

JEWEL Stingy, retired gentleman. Someone would like to hear from you, but not me. Confidentially, I don't desire contact, and intend to delay my happiness.

SAVAGE Right you are, muscled maiden; your duty is to protect me, not to think of yourself. Lift me out of the damp and change the bedding. My, the way the rubber sheet underneath has slipped to one side, make sure you anchor it properly this time. Ready!
(*He holds out his arms for* JEWEL *to lift him out*)

JEWEL Say "Into your arms."

SAVAGE Into your arms, attractive member.

JEWEL I give the finest personalized assistance to help you.
(*She takes him in her arms and puts him in a chair. Then she goes to the cupboard*)

SAVAGE Stop what you're doing!

JEWEL Why?

SAVAGE Feed me my eggs first.

JEWEL First from what?

SAVAGE Let the sheets rot. (JEWEL *sighs and cracks his eggs into the dish. She feeds him. He eats with relish. His face drips with yolk*) Clean me up.

JEWEL   You have a very pretty napkin for your mouth.

SAVAGE   The egg's dried and you're more thorough.

JEWEL   I'll dampen a washcloth.

SAVAGE   Someday you'll be sorry, sorry you weren't nicer to me. Someday when I receive five hundred and twelve photos and find real love, then you'll be sorry.

JEWEL   Cupid's destiny seeks you in every mail. I don't suppose you've ever heard of self-introduction?

SAVAGE   Speak freely.

JEWEL   I am.

SAVAGE   Introduce yourself.

JEWEL   Kiss me and cry no more. I'm a glamazon and anything goes. Power packed and best in action is Jewel.

SAVAGE   That's why I hired you. Your department is beyond words. However, I wish I could go beyond—to do—

JEWEL   Try not to slide off that chair while I make everything nice.

SAVAGE (*Petulantly*)   Jan is all business.

JEWEL   You're playing with fire.

SAVAGE   She's naughty but nice.

JEWEL   An amateur!
(*She removes the sheet from the bed*)

SAVAGE   Puts on a show you'll never forget. Say, what's that?

JEWEL   What's what?

SAVAGE You've pocketed something.

JEWEL I haven't.

SAVAGE Let me make sure.

JEWEL Sure of what?

SAVAGE That you haven't taken something out from under the mattress.

JEWEL Is there something under there? I'll look.

SAVAGE No, no, I was only pulling your leg. Don't look.

JEWEL We had a verbal agreement, no secrets; have you gone back on your word?

SAVAGE Oooo, these are terrible eggs, take them away.

JEWEL Have you gone back on your word?

SAVAGE I suppose I have. My word is portable, you know.

JEWEL What do you mean?

SAVAGE Don't be angry, *please!*

JEWEL Explain.

SAVAGE (*Slyly*) My word is lightweight; I can take it back with no strain at all.

JEWEL (*She starts to look under the mattress*) Ah-ha, what's this?

SAVAGE Common sense, that's what it is. Costs only cents to operate.

JEWEL (*She pulls out a microphone and a headset*) Hot-dawg!

SAVAGE Don't take it away, little honey-pot, I need it.

JEWEL Where's the rest of it?

SAVAGE Under the bed.

JEWEL You've dripped through. You've wet it.
(*She pulls a tiny tape recorder out from under the bed*)

SAVAGE It's precision engineered, renders the same functions as a, I've forgotten what. Faithfully records, perfect for recording interviews, and—and—

JEWEL Dance nocturne?
(*She does a whirling turn*)

SAVAGE Costing five times as much, captures the magic of speech —ingenious—records, plays back, erases.

JEWEL Okay, play something, convince me.

SAVAGE (*He takes the apparatus in his lap and fiddles with it. Finally he gets it going. The tape hisses like steam; then like a steady drip, drip of water.* SAVAGE *speaks, his voice under seven wagons of cotton*) The secret is you demanded them. She made astonishing statements: Bubbles Darlene used a dirty towel and left a ring around the tub. I got wet too at my navel, who's to blame? She, Pepper Powell, sister of Dick, took my Dick with the astonishing ability to relieve pain, to shrink without surgery. Cherry Knight strode in to say, "Jubilee of joy be with you." Flame Fury seared Gay Dawn who was trying to come up. You are Gray, Miss Gay, I ventured. Dawn was to be shot at Dawn, I preempted my load. "Shot your bolt," she gaily cried. Fifty-foot adult and let 'er roll! You don't need a projector. See sparkling lifelike, fast or slow motion.

JEWEL Turn it off.

SAVAGE Then I may keep it?

JEWEL   Innocent fun. Why be lonely?

SAVAGE   An extra bonus for you, daughter of Eve.
(*He plays a fanfare on an imaginary horn*)

JEWEL   I don't care about your age. I hope you meet the kind of woman you hope to meet. There must be a woman somewhere screaming to meet you. If you meet that kind of woman maybe you'll stop.

SAVAGE   You have a nicely curved smile. You're not only an employee, you're a real friend. Don't worry, I'll take care of you someday.

JEWEL   (*All broken up*)   I must finish making the bed.
(*She resumes making the bed*)

SAVAGE   The extra bonus is. (*Weak singing fanfare*) A luxurious negligée to complete the most feminine set ever. Specifically designed to enticingly hide and yet show. Sheer black lace nylon, jet black, in extra large.

JEWEL   (*Turns on him savagely*)   Extra large is not sheer enchantment! Save your bedroom fashions for sizes thirty-two to forty.

SAVAGE   Would you prefer a trio of love pledge panties? They come in stretchable nylon bespangled with rhinestones.

JEWEL   (*Crying, she throws her arms around* SAVAGE's *neck*)
You're so good, so very kind, but one man tells another.

SAVAGE   No one shall know. This time my word is permanent.

JEWEL   Dare I? (*Bravely*) Why not meet the sun halfway!

SAVAGE   Bravo, brutiful, now is the time to display that powerfully developed form. I'm tired.

JEWEL   Bed's made. Do you want that thing back under the mattress?

SAVAGE   I'll hide it myself. Gonna play a trick on Jan.

JEWEL   Come on, Corrupt dear, back to bed.

SAVAGE   Some day I'm gonna have me a custom made bed with lots of room for wet fun.

JEWEL   You can afford it. You can afford a whole field of beds. Why don't you get what you want?

SAVAGE *(Shakes his head dreamily)*   I just don't know.
    (JEWEL carries him in her arms. She walks around the room a few times)

JEWEL   At my risk, in your home, a walk around the room.

SAVAGE   Nice. So nice to be pressed against your genuine heavy equipment; it's really ringside, isn't it?

JEWEL   Say the word and anything goes, Corrupt dear. Tangle with the best.

SAVAGE   Age forbids. A milder tonic for me.

JEWEL   Jan?
    (She puts him on the bed)

SAVAGE   What she lacks in skill, she makes up in merchandising.

JEWEL   Want anything else to eat?

SAVAGE *(Winks lasciviously)*   Oo-la-la.

JEWEL   Here's your reading material. *(She spreads the magazines on the bed as before.* SAVAGE *opens a wide one on the pillow and puts his nose in the centerfold. He is lying on his belly)*   Can't see much that way.

SAVAGE *(Mumbles)*   Let me be the judge of that. It's a double delight no matter how you look at it.

JEWEL   Well then, please excuse this staggering hunk of earthi-
ness.

SAVAGE   While you're out there, see if I've received my new talent
portfolio. Scram!

JEWEL *(Under her breath)*   Sucker.
    (She exits and the lights dim)

Blackout

The scene takes place in the kitchen of CORRUPT SAVAGE'S *apartment.* JAN, JEWEL *and* JORDAN *are seated around a small white worktable; they are smoking pot. There is a bowl of salad with lettuce, carrots, tomatoes and green pepper, on the table.* JAN *is giggly,* JORDAN *horny, and* JEWEL *is withdrawn and a trifle paranoiac.*

JORDAN   Well?
   (*He takes a carrot and breaks it in half*)

JAN (*Giggling*)   Well? Well, well, well, well, well.

JORDAN (*He hands* JAN *a piece of carrot*)   Good for your eyes. I want you to see at night. I want you to open those big beautiful baby blues and find out where the old fart hides his loot.

JAN (*Takes the carrot and munches on it*)   Probably keeps it in the bank.

JEWEL (*Eating a slice of tomato*)   Uh-uh! Not him. Wouldn't be surprised if he swallowed it in a plastic bag and shit it out every Sunday to pay my wages.

JORDAN (*Lighting a reefer*)   Here, have a drag. (*Offers it to* JEWEL. *She takes it and drags a long, deep one*) Up to now we haven't got a clue. Ladies, I think you stink. In fact, I believe you're not following instructions.

JAN (*Takes a drag of* JEWEL's *pot and speaks, trying not to let the smoke out*)   I am following instructions. I kiss him, and touch him, and ask him to do dirty, nasty things, and I use his toothbrush and towel and warm his feet, and kiss his toes one by one, and, oh golly, he says I'm the best in the business, and he's gonna give me a diploma and a letter of recommendation.

JEWEL (*Daintily holding a lettuce leaf aloft, shaking it so that drops of water fall off*) Remember, you're just a figment of his imagination, and mine.

JORDAN And mine. He's just using you. He's like us. Wants to get! Wants to get without paying. I'll make him pay.

JEWEL Through the nose!

JORDAN Through the eyes, ears, mouth and the South of him! Through Jan dear. (*He caresses her*) And when he's through with her he'll be finished, done in, a panting, pitiful old man with just a bowl of soft, hot cream of farina to dip his finger into.

JEWEL I'll take the spoons, they're gold-plated.

JAN So are his teeth. They feel so heavy when they bite into me. He likes to bite me and I ask him to stop because the human bite is poisonous. I have poison all over my skin and my clothes and my hair. It makes me so mad to be bitten at.

JEWEL I'll take his teeth too. They make him look like a donkey anyway. Ever heard him bray?
(*JORDAN laughs*)

JAN He only brays when he makes love. He taught me how to bray. (*She brays*) He says it's a sign of passion, real passion, when partners in love make animal sounds. He pulls his lips up and makes a terrible racket. It reminds me of a story my mother used to read to me called *The Musicians of Bremen*. All these animals got together and stood on each others' shoulders and brayed and meowed and barked and crowed and what not to scare the robbers in the house. The robbers in the house.
(*She giggles*)

JORDAN Sounds like he's on to us. Why should he have chosen that sound?

JEWEL He's foxy, that wolf. But he can't frighten me. I've heard everything there is to hear. I've heard him gurgling like a sewer, laughing like a hyena, crying like a virgin in a cathouse, cooing like a pig's foot buried in sauerkraut, screaming like a man who can't find his lost limb but still feels pain in it.
(*She smokes some more pot*)

JAN (*Jealous*) He never did that for me. He never made me hear his sound effects. (*She munches loudly on a carrot and anything else on the table*) He never tries to amuse me at all.

JORDAN He despises you. What are you to him?

JAN He calls me Jan.

JEWEL He calls *me* his little honey-pot.

JAN No wonder—you're sticky and you look like a pot. You look like a pot that stayed in the fire too long. You've got a dirty bottom, you're bruised and bashed in, your handle is so hot you burn the flesh right off, and it smells and you smell and there's nothing in you, nothing at all, nothing at all, nothing ... (*She weeps*) ... nothing, nothing but a charred bone—the remains of a poor meal—a poor, cheap meal evaporated—floating in the clouds.

JEWEL Speak for yourself, Jan. You're the one in the clouds. Food for the gods, eh! The gods who keep their mouths open waiting for you to enter them? The gods who don't bite? The gods who don't swallow? No substance to you or your gods!

JAN (*Goes over to* JORDAN *for comfort*) I don't believe in gods, I don't believe in men. I don't believe in people. You're right, Jordan, everybody wants to get!

JORDAN Getting and spending we lay waste our powers. (*Pats her head as if she is the child she is*) But it's only human, Jan dear.

Only human to coax and pull the donkey to where we want to go. (*Takes the carrot and dangles it in front of her nose*) Only human . . . (*He gets up and makes her follow the carrot*) . . . to show it what it wants—to get it going, and then—jump on, to make the donkey carry us. You're the carrot, baby, and Corrupt Savage has enough back on him to carry us all. He may be old, but he makes an excellent beast of burden.

JAN   But he can't hardly get out of bed. I don't follow you.

JEWEL   You weren't hired for your brains. You were hired to enter his world and yank him out of it. (*She gets tough and yanks* JAN *around*) There are mountains in his room, dangerously high mountains, and lakes, great big round deep lakes with a whirlpool in each one. You're the lady in the lake.

JORDAN   The lady who rises out of the depths and lures tired, parched, hot old donkeys to their death.

JEWEL   Right down the drain with the rest of the hair!

JAN   I can't do it. I can't hurt him. I'm sort of his friend.

JORDAN   You don't have to stop being his friend. After we get away with the lettuce. (*He stuffs a huge handful of lettuce into his pocket*) You can stay with him if you want to and hustle for him, you can doll him up like a regular pimp and give him the take, and when he drops dead, you can stuff him and make a fancy pillow out of his shapeless shaggy showcase, and shove him under your ass when the customers want to go deeper. And you won't mind, because that old fat pillow will have you in its spell, softening each thrust, drinking in each protein spurt that leaks out of you. But you'll be friends, the human blotter and you—friends to the bitter, bitten end!

JAN   You, you're just a runt!

JORDAN   And you, Jan dear, are just a cunt! Just.

JEWEL   It's his fault we're fighting among ourselves. Come on, Jan, chin up, we've got a job to do and we might as well attend to it. Can't back out now. Corrupt is on to something. He's keeping a tape recorder under his mattress.

JAN   So?

JEWEL   He has evidence. We must destroy the evidence. At least I think it's evidence. It's spoken in code.

JORDAN   He's clever all right, but if A follows B, I believe that Mr. Corrupt Savage will relinquish his fortune, cheerfully, even if Jewel has to beat it out of him . . . (*Ominously*) . . . drop by ruby-red drop. How about it, Jewel, is the old boy kinky or isn't he?

JEWEL   I haven't prepared my report on that yet, Jordan, but if you think I should order a whip, I will.

JORDAN   See if you can't engage him in harmless kinky talk. Converse with him about matters of flagellation and Dalmation.

JEWEL   Don't you mean damnation?

JORDAN   I say what I mean and I mean what I say—Dalmation!

JEWEL   Okay. Then what?

JORDAN   Loosen his tongue, arouse his ardor. If things don't work out, I have an alternate plan. Something that will be strictly between Mr. Corrupt Savage and myself.

Blackout

The bedroom of MR. CORRUPT SAVAGE. *It is totally dark.*

SAVAGE   I'm all alone in the dark and yet I see magnificent unre-
touched pictures. I tingle at these pictures that can't be obtained
anywhere else. My response is beyond my wildest expectations.
Let's face it, Corrupt, you'll never take advantage of the money-
back guarantee. You don't have to. (*He chuckles*) Now I have a
treat in store for myself again. Push-button memory isn't everything. Door's locked. Miss Jewel Glass kept at bay. Ah, here they
are in the automatic feeder. Come to me, Rose Red, in your most
daring, most revealing pose. (*Familiar poses by Rose Red are projected onto the opposite wall by a slide projector from the bed of*
CORRUPT SAVAGE) Christ, Rose you're the thorniest! Lethal rosebuds (*He makes sucking sounds*) taste so good. (*Suddenly the
room is in total darkness again as the projector plug pulls out*)
Damn plug! In, in damn plug. (*The projector works again.
Another slide of Rose appears on the wall. Rose is shown with a
whip*) Ah, there it is! Buxom bombshell be mine. Destroy me.
Explode in my face, ooze milk, float those rosebuds, feed me,
flood me, smother me. Where are you going to put it?
   (*There is loud knocking on the door*)

JEWEL   Mr. Savage, are you napping?

SAVAGE   No, I'm nipping.

JEWEL   I thought I heard you talking in your sleep.

SAVAGE   You did, you did.

JEWEL   That's dangerous. I'm glad I stopped you.

SAVAGE   They all are. They stop me and they're glad of it.

JEWEL   Can I get you something?

SAVAGE   Go away.

JEWEL   I have something for you.

SAVAGE (*With joy*)   The new talent portfolio?

JEWEL   No, Jan's here.

SAVAGE (*Groans*)   She's too real right now. Tell her to wait.

JEWEL   Okay Corrupt, you're the boss. Shout when you want me.

SAVAGE (*Sings*)   I'll shout, sister, shout, I'll tell the whole world what it's all about.

JEWEL   Every nation in the whole world has a flag. I love the way flags hang and blow. When I was a little girl I knew every flag by heart.

SAVAGE   Well, keep your eyes peeled, baby, there's a flag in the field now that's head and shoulders above all others.

JEWEL   You!

SAVAGE   Red and purple above a split crest.

JEWEL   Silence! I suspect the deepest secret of your secret soul.

SAVAGE   Hit home! Hit home!

JEWEL   One day I shall bleed it out of you, torturous drop by torturous drop.

SAVAGE (*In awe*)   Majesty!

JEWEL   I am going to punish others . . . and you shall only watch!

SAVAGE   Refined torture at its best. Inflict it upon me, sweet tyrant.

JEWEL   Let me in.

SAVAGE   I'm too stiff to get to the door. Go speak to Jan while I limber up.

JEWEL   Mr. Savage, when I return I expect you to strip yourself before my royal eyes.

SAVAGE   Bring the little electric heater with you.

JEWEL   Certainly, Corrupt.

SAVAGE   I can't get too much of a good thing; relentless debasement, and abject suffering, now and forever as hard as you can!

JEWEL   I'll force you to respond by dealing with you.

SAVAGE   As it suits your fancy, oh mistress. (JEWEL's *retreating footsteps are heard*) Now she thinks I'm a masochist and in her power. She has another think coming. She will expose her evil plans with my capable assistance. I know she wants my fortune and so does Jan. I'll go along with it and have some fun. Adult fun! (*The projector is turned off and regular lights go on.* SAVAGE *reaches under his pillow and pulls out a wig. He tries to put it on, but it keeps slipping off his head and out of his hands*) Hmm, seems to have a life of its own. Wants to get back to the original owner; I'd let it go, but I can't believe my wig prefers a horse's ass to my head. (*He jams it back under the pillow and calls loudly*) Jewel! Let's put the show on the road! Jewel!
   (*Footsteps are heard outside the door and then a crash.* JEWEL *smashes the door in and steps through it. Immediately following her is* JAN, *dressed in a rubber deep-sea-diving outfit, fins and all, spear, etc. She makes feeble swimming movements with her hands as she walks forward*)

JEWEL   Howd'ya like them apples, Savage?

SAVAGE   Quick, the sex-o-meter! Have you forgotten it?
   (JEWEL *takes a kind of grip-o-meter with attached ther-*

mometer and bell out of her apron pocket, hands it to
SAVAGE. *He starts squeezing*)

JAN   I'd love to go underwater spear-fishing in Yucatan with you.
I'd love to go underwater spear-fishing with you in Yucatan.
*(She stops at the foot of the bed, makes several inept thrusts
with her spear, and bumps and grinds)*

SAVAGE *(He squeezes the meter as hard as he can)*   Nope, no, go,
baby, it don't mean a thing to me, but don't give up. (JEWEL *and*
JAN *leave*) If they only knew how easy it could be.
*(JEWEL comes through the broken door again. She then
makes an announcement)*

JEWEL   The Fire Dance!
(JAN enters dancing, dressed in scarves of orange and red)

SAVAGE   I can put that fire out! I know how to. Jewel, you pump
and I'll direct the hose.

JEWEL   Are you excited?

SAVAGE   False alarm. (JEWEL *shrugs her shoulders and marches
out with* JAN *following*) It can't be the fault of the meter; it's
worked before.
(JEWEL re-enters and announces)

JEWEL   How to use a sunlamp! (JAN *enters, rolling a sunlamp in
front of her. She is fully dressed in skirt and blouse, black hose
and five-inch heels. She is wearing a mask and long black leather
gloves. She stops somewhere midstage and* JEWEL *brings a chair
to her. She strips, starting with the gloves, but leaves on a black
waist cincher, black bra, and her hose and shoes. She takes various poses, using the chair as she would a man: she is supposedly
getting a sun-ray treatment)* The little lady is a sun worshiper.
Notice the nice tan. If you wish, she can administer a tanning
too. Though your hide be thick as an elephant's she promises to
get under your skin.

SAVAGE (*Grips the sex-o-meter*) Sorry, doesn't ring a bell.

JEWEL Honey, are you tired of not getting what you want?

SAVAGE I thought you were a hot promoter.

JEWEL Breathe easy, daddy, your troubles are over.

SAVAGE I wish I could believe that. (JEWEL *motions to* JAN *and they leave together*) Monkey business and stage props! That Jewel lady knows exactly what I want and yet she rings in a fringe area. Last week it was *Pagan Fables of a Human Horse*, told with the aid of bit and bridle. She thinks me complicated, and yet I'm a simple fellow. (JEWEL *enters alone*) Has she gone?

JEWEL She has.

SAVAGE Did you pay her?

JEWEL I did.

SAVAGE What did she say?

JEWEL She said: "If I'm not in, my answering service will take the message."

SAVAGE You told her you'd call her again?

JEWEL Yes.

SAVAGE You're jealous of her, that's why you give her the wrong get-ups.

JEWEL Are you ready to be turned?

SAVAGE Damn ready! And this time powder me with cornstarch, I perspire too much.

Blackout

SCENE 4

The bedroom again. MR. CORRUPT SAVAGE *is seated in a rocking chair.* JORDAN *comes in swiftly and glances back through the door to see if he is being followed.*

JORDAN   Mr. Savage, I have something for you.

SAVAGE   I do not know you.

JORDAN   Jordan's the name. You know me now.

SAVAGE   Who sent you?

JORDAN   No one. I am here on my own.

SAVAGE   What do you want with me?

JORDAN   Everyone, whether rich or poor, should have a will.

SAVAGE   I have a will.

JORDAN   Not a strong will.

SAVAGE   A will to win.

JORDAN   A willy-nilly.

SAVAGE   A willful will.

JORDAN   A will or won't.

SAVAGE   A will.

JORDAN   A wilt!

SAVAGE   Why are you attacking me?

JORDAN   Want to know the ins and outs in simple language?

SAVAGE   Yes.
        (JORDAN *takes a sixty-four-page booklet out of his pocket*)

JORDAN   Take this. (*He hands the booklet to* SAVAGE) *Wills: How
to Make and How to Break Them.*

SAVAGE   I'm not about to die. (*Whispers*) Not about to die.

JORDAN   Will!

SAVAGE   Won't!

JORDAN   Prove it! I'll wait.

SAVAGE   I still consider myself a red-blooded adult who wants to
love, live and laugh.

JORDAN   Even those kind die.

SAVAGE   They die in the future.

JORDAN   Wipe out all debts now!

SAVAGE   I owe nothing, I am happy most of the time, I like pets, I
like city life, I like country life, I've been in love. My name is
Corrupt Savage. I've spoken to you confidentially although you're
not the Help Company.

JORDAN   I can help you assemble artificial lures at home.

SAVAGE   What do you want?

JORDAN   Adopt me and make me the beneficiary of your will.

SAVAGE   I like you, you're outspoken. What kind of girls do you
like?

JORDAN Burly girls; and you sir?

SAVAGE Perhaps, perhaps.

JORDAN I can help you publish your book. Join our successful authors.

SAVAGE Perhaps, perhaps.

JORDAN Play guitar in seven days!

SAVAGE Perhaps, perhaps.

JORDAN Be a fingerprint expert.

SAVAGE I have some song ideas too, but no, no, you are right—

JORDAN About what?

SAVAGE I have a premonition that I don't even have time for the one-week course.

JORDAN Desperate? You are surrounded by strangers. Let me be your son.

SAVAGE You don't appeal to me.

JORDAN But you are at the end.

SAVAGE I am holding the end and I am turning the rope very slowly. It is your turn to jump.

JORDAN A girl's game.

SAVAGE We are interlopers, but nevertheless it is your turn to jump.

JORDAN I'll try.
      (SAVAGE *turns an imaginary rope.* JORDAN *gets ready to*

*jump and then jumps up and down as if he is jumping rope.
He trips and hurts his ankle)*

SAVAGE   Missed!

JORDAN   Interference. Someone got in the way.

SAVAGE   Not someone, me. I pulled the rope tight and made you
miss. The ender is in control.
(Laughs)

JORDAN   Have you ever heard of a steady ender?

SAVAGE   No.

JORDAN   A steady ender never gets a chance to jump, keeps turning till everyone goes home. Know how you got to be a steady
ender?

SAVAGE   What's your considered opinion?

JORDAN   That you are suffering from a bad heart, and cannot under any circumstances be allowed to jump.

SAVAGE   I can jump whenever I wish, I am active, active—
*(SAVAGE rises from his chair and jumps in a sickening way:
out of breath, clumsily. Finally he falls to the floor)*

JORDAN   See, I told you! Need some help?

SAVAGE   Call Jewel.

JORDAN   I want your signature and your name. Here are the
papers.
(He hands a folio of papers to the sick SAVAGE on the floor)

SAVAGE *(Spits on the papers)*   I'd rather die.

JORDAN   The ink is waterproof, Mr. Savage; your spit won't blur
the script. Oh, and here is a pen.

SAVAGE (*Weakly calls* JEWEL) Jewel!
> (JEWEL *comes in as if she had been waiting right outside the door*)

JEWEL You called, sir?

SAVAGE Lift me onto the bed.

JEWEL Okay.
> (*She does so without warmth*)

SAVAGE Jewel, this man wants my life or my money.

JEWEL I know.

SAVAGE Are you the witness?

JEWEL Yes dear. I do and say what graduates say.

SAVAGE What do you mean?

JEWEL Graduates say: I am doing very well in my spare time.

SAVAGE I was a fool to think you really liked me.

JEWEL If you liked me you would have been generous.

JORDAN We've all provided practical experience for each other.

SAVAGE You can't force free gifts.

JORDAN If you don't sign we'll raid the premises anyway.
> (JAN *runs in breathless*)

JAN Mr. Savage, I have something for you. I picked it up accidentally with my costumes.

JEWEL Give it to me.

JAN It isn't for you.

SAVAGE They promised that no salesman would call. Give me my package, it's the long-awaited new talent portfolio. A last look.

JEWEL Okay, give it to him. Let his lecherous eyes bug.

JAN Here you are, sweet old man. Do you want me to turn the pages?

SAVAGE Do you mean it?

JAN I can be false to no man.

SAVAGE Sit here and hold it close. I don't see very well.
(JAN *tears the package open and looks at the magazine with* SAVAGE. JEWEL *motions to* JORDAN *and they go out*)

JAN Is it nice?

SAVAGE This is where loneliness ends. The milk of human kindness.

JAN No more hilarious situations, just you and me.

SAVAGE Personalized! I want to give you all I own. Not because you deserve it, but because I always make last-minute decisions and also, the album we are perusing is an especially exciting one.

JAN Thank you, dear.
(*She kisses him*)

SAVAGE You are forever artlessly gowned in my mind.

JAN Thank you, dear.
(*Kisses him again*)

SAVAGE I believe that I am now ready to be privately released.

JAN Really?

SAVAGE   On this bed of pain.

JAN   Now?

SAVAGE   For the last time. I know what I want and you've got it.

JAN   But any minute now my business manager will burst in.

SAVAGE   Screw him girlie. The price is high and the moon is high.

JAN   But Jewel and Jordan might—

SAVAGE   Terrific! Hot! Young! Luscious!
    (*He embraces her*)

JAN   Help! Oh help!
    (*He pins her beneath him*)

SAVAGE   Wow! Wow! Grrrr!
    (CORRUPT SAVAGE *suddenly goes limp, but* JAN *is trapped. The voices of* JEWEL *and* JORDAN *are heard coming to the rescue. There is a blackout. Sounds of thunder come from the tape. There is a general confusion of sound*)

Curtain

The bedroom. MR. CORRUPT SAVAGE *laid out on the bed. The rest of the cast is turning the room upside down, looking for money, jewels, etc.* JEWEL *pulls the tape recorder out from under the mattress. She starts it going.*

TAPE RECORDER   You're all under arrest! (*All arrest their activities sharply and gasp with surprise*) Line up quickly! This is Corrupt Savage speaking, coming to you from the great beyond. Go on, line up, no pushing. Size places will do. (*All line up with much measuring of height and pushing*) You are about to hear my last will and testament, but first I must be properly mourned. Jewel, you are to intone the dirge. (JEWEL *shakes her head*) Reluctant? Then repeat after me, with expression. NIGHT AND DAY HE PERUSED AMERICA'S PICTURE MAGAZINES FOR ENTERTAINMENT.

JEWEL   Night and day he perused America's picture magazines for entertainment.

TAPE RECORDER   HE IGNORED *PEEPERS' CHOICE* FOR *INSIDE STORY,* AND FOUND IT NAUGHTY BUT NICE. SKYSCRAPER HEELS, APPROXIMATELY FIVE INCHES HIGH, GORED HIS PATENT LEATHER SOUL.

JEWEL   He, he—

TAPE RECORDER   HE WOULD TRY ANYTHING ONCE: *THE MAGIC KEY TO LOVE AND SEX* IN EIGHT VOLUMES FOR ONLY $4.98. CURIOUS FROM THE BOTTOM OF HIS HEART, HE READ COMPLETE INSTRUCTIONS.

JEWEL   I read those out loud to him.

TAPE RECORDER BUT THE MECHANISM WAS FAULTY. EVEN DONALDA JORDAN, SPORTING A CIRCUMFERENCE OF FORTY-ONE INCHES AND ADORING SINATRA, PRESLEY, MONROE, AND SIAMESE CATS, WHICH SHE RAISED FOR LOVE OR MONEY, COULDN'T FILL THE BILL. HE WANTED TO SHOUT: "OWN ME," OR "YOU'LL NEVER KNOW WHAT I HAVE TO OFFER"; COVER TO COVER THEY COULDN'T WAIT, THEY FLIPPED OVER BACKWARDS FOR MORE INTERESTING SHOTS. FEMALE FIGHTERS KNOCKED HIM OUT, AFTER DECLARING IN "CAPS": WE LIKE MEN FRIENDS. HE SPECIFIED AND HE RECEIVED. THE ONLY MEANS OF ACCESS TO HIS LIFE WAS BY SUBSCRIPTION ONLY.

JEWEL Just like him to hog the whole dirge.

TAPE RECORDER Jewel, turn me off, turn me off, turn me off. Wait! I meant to tell you and Jan who's been so kind to me. I meant to tell you where the money is.

JEWEL He's going to tell.

TAPE RECORDER In the basement where you store the magazines you'll find a batch from 1956 to 1958; there's money between each page. I have a habit of paying off the photos according to appreciation. You'll have to look carefully so as not to miss any of it, and please, when you come to the more expensive pages, say goodbye for me. Say: "He's tantalizing himself in the breathtaking sky blue, and is no longer yours alone!"
  (JEWEL *turns off the tape recorder, and shrugs her shoulders*)

JORDAN Maybe there's life in the old boy yet.

JEWEL Dead or alive, he'll fog your mirror for you. Come on.
  (JORDAN *holds the door open and then all go out. We see a blue light on the bed and* SAVAGE—*who smiles*)

Curtain

Softly, and Consider the Nearness

CAST

NONA   A lady who lives alone; she is between
                              thirty and fifty.

T.V.   A floor model.

SNEAKTHIEF   A sneakthief.

(To be played in the style of a children's play. T.V. moves and wears his T.V. like the Tin Man in The Wizard of Oz. *The movement may be choreographed, mimelike.)*

Scene: NONA's *living room; it contains an easy chair and a huge T.V.* NONA *enters, changes from her business clothes, and greets the T.V.*

NONA   Hello baby. I'm here. (*She caresses the set*) It was a long day without you, but I kept looking out the window by my desk imagining it was your screen. What a gray day, and I couldn't even adjust the contrast. (*She turns a few knobs and puts the set on*) You shine up the whole room. (*There is a high piercing signal*) I'll fix that.
   (*She fiddles with the antennae and knobs and goes behind the set*)

T.V.   Don't we get a better picture together? For a while I thought you were going to let me grow cold.

NONA   You are always in my heart, and as long as I live you will remain there.

T.V.   Trapped!

NONA   Don't feel that way.

T.V.   I have no choice in the matter. I stay where I am put.

NONA   You are the object of my desire.

T.V.   I think that you delight in the fact that I am an object. My destiny is your will.

NONA   You're fighting your attraction for me, from your plastic knobs right down to your leatherette finish.

T.V.   When I first came to your home my features were my qualifications, but now you are using them against me.

NONA   Are you going to be difficult?

T.V.   Yes. That is the way I am built.

NONA   I know about that. I know how to shut you up too. (*She stoops down to pull out the plug*) You'll never say another word.

T.V.   Before you silence me, remember, I bring you your lovers. I parade them past you for your own pleasure. I ask no more than to see and be seen.

NONA   What do you want, a medal?

T.V.   Listen to me, I tell the truth.

NONA   I don't like documentaries.

T.V.   If only I knew what you really wanted.

NONA   What if you did know? What could you do about it?

T.V.   Nothing. I can only transmit the messages of others.

NONA   But I am free to interpret those messages.

T.V.   Not all messages speak of love.

NONA   I choose carefully, in the T.V. guide. There is a short description of all programs.

T.V. (*Resentful*)   I owe my life to you.

NONA (*Conciliatory*)   I owe mine to you. Do you still feel trapped?

T.V.   We are in reciprocal debt. Does that mean we are in love?

NONA   It means we are together.
        (*There is a pause*)

T.V. What if some day you view on my screen a lady, like yourself, being strangled. Would you blame me?

NONA The idea wouldn't have come to you if you hadn't thought of it.

T.V. Must I remind you that I have no thoughts?

NONA Cold outside, but inside you're glowing and warm.

T.V. The longer I'm on, the hotter I get.

NONA You won't burn out.

T.V. Others have with less use.

NONA You're such an excellent set I'd like to kiss you, but I don't want to get lipstick on my furniture.

T.V. You've got me where you want me.

NONA Right between channels.

T.V. I have an itch.

NONA Where?

T.V. I'm not sure. Scratch me vertical and then scratch me horizontal, that ought to do it.

NONA Like man and wife. (*She pulls the T.V. antennae in and out, trying to get a better picture*) There, I like the way you're coming in, I don't want to lose you.

T.V. You couldn't if you tried.

NONA Do you hear that?
(*There is the sound of* SNEAKTHIEF)

T.V.   The sound of electricity crackling through my wires.

NONA   Something else.

T.V.   It's nothing, you were imagining it.

NONA   That is very possible. I don't know why I'm so jumpy.

T.V.   Use a doctor's remedy, the kind that can be purchased without a doctor's prescription at the drugstore.

NONA   Don't send me away.

T.V.   Just a short trip for instant relief.

NONA   You sound so, so . . .

T.V.   Commercial?

NONA   Yes.

T.V.   If only I could hold you, the way I hold the sound and the picture.

NONA   How comforting that would be.

T.V.   Your body, all cuddled up, might fit into my chassis, and your face is certainly true-Vue.

NONA   What would I say? Everyone's eyes would be on me!

T.V.   You are never at a loss for words.

NONA   I need encouragement.

T.V.   Say anything that comes to you, but include a vast audience. Greet them. You have been invited into their homes.

NONA   Yes, I am their guest. They want to be in my company. I need rehearsal.

T.V.   Be spontaneous.

NONA   Okay, but stop me if I get out of line. I'm liable to say things I mean.

T.V.   I can't stop you, I can only start you.

NONA   Okay then. (*She smiles broadly*) Ladies and gentlemen. I am here tonight because . . .

T.V.   Go on.

NONA   I am here tonight because I have nowhere else to go.

T.V.   Tell them why.

NONA   Because I am a . . .

T.V.   A what?

NONA   I am afraid to describe myself.

T.V.   You don't have to, they see you.

NONA   They see that I am living alone? That I have no friends, no family?

T.V.   They see a star in the making.

NONA   I want to hide behind a cloud.

T.V.   Continue your speech.

NONA   Ladies and gentlemen, I am here tonight because I have been asked by a close friend to appeal to you, but I am not particularly appealing and so you will have to love me for myself.

T.V.   Speak about what they mean to you.

NONA   I wish they weren't there.

T.V.   Try to reach them.

NONA (*She makes a few false starts as if she is about to speak, and then does*)   Hello, is it you? It is so nice of you to tune in on me. I have been waiting some time for your invitation. I shall send you some lovely autographed photos of mine. Please be good enough to send your name and address to Post Office Box 237, Post Office Times Square, New York. Do enclose a dollar for the photos, please. And thank you very much for your remittance. All the best. And don't forget: Post Office Box 237, Post Office Times Square.

T.V.   We belong together. There must be a way to enclose you, before I go dead.

NONA   Dearest, a limited engagement is better than none at all.

T.V.   With you checking my tubes, I could go on forever.

NONA (*She goes to the back of the T.V. set and starts pulling out tubes and switching them around. There is an explosion, and smoke, and the smell of smoke.* NONA, *terribly shaken, tries to right things, but she can't. She starts thumbing through the Yellow Pages for a repairman*)   I can't remember who the company recommends. It's all my fault. What'll I do now? (*She finally fixes the set herself*) You know, for a while I thought I'd lost you.

T.V.   Poor girl.

NONA   And I thought of all the things I would have liked to say to you but didn't.

T.V   You can say them now.

NONA (*Choked with emotion*)   I can't.

T.V.   Tell me, would you have replaced me with another set, if . . .

NONA   Oh no! I would have lived with the memory of you.

T.V.   The pictures I project on my screen are the same pictures that flash across any T.V. Your memories are not yours alone. They are shared, they are mirrored; and when they catch the sun, your memories sear and burn, turn to ash, and you have nothing.

NONA   My memories of our moments together are indoor events; no sun enters this room. What I have with you no one else has. Frankly, do you realize what our relationship has become?

T.V.   Illicit? Are you guilty?

NONA   A little, certainly. Those times I went to bed with you.

T.V.   You heard my voice first thing in the morning.

NONA   I need that kind of thing. A woman needs comforting.

T.V.   Ah, I see it all now, you love me for my adaptability, for my eye on the world, and my heart in the lap.

NONA   You are mine alone. I offer you nothing and you are mine. The purchase made you mine. No one can refute it. We'll grow old together. I own you, I own you, I own you!

T.V.   Well, I for one am glad of it. I went up in smoke but here I am good as new again. What happened when I was out cold?

NONA   I touched parts of you I would never have dared touch, and then I pulled out a few cold tubes.

T.V.   I didn't feel a thing.

NONA   I nearly fainted. I hoped against hope that you could be fixed right away. I attached something to your main tube, thought it might brighten you a bit.

T.V.   I don't brighten easily.
       (*There is the sound of* SNEAKTHIEF)

NONA   Did you hear something?

T.V   It might be the wind.

NONA   No, someone!

T.V.   I'm sure it's nothing or no one.
        (*There is a pause*)

NONA   When you went up in smoke, I was about to embrace you.
Are you sure that you didn't cause yourself to explode?

T.V.   I tried too hard, maybe that was it.

NONA   Isn't everything allowable between us?

T.V.   Things allowable between people often come between them.

NONA   Let's not argue. I'm so sleepy.
        (*She lays her head on the T.V. There are a few seconds of
        tender silence. The T.V. speaks first, like baby-talk in a
        dream. The lights dim*)

T.V.   What's my little bird going to feed itself tonight?

NONA   Only what's under its dear little beak.

T.V.   And what's under its dear little beak?

NONA   Well, nothing yet. The little boys who found the little bird
and who don't want it to die have gone to ask their mothers for
crusts of bread. I am wrapped in the dirty handkerchief of one
of those boys and am smothering in his pocket.

T.V.   You can't get out.

NONA   I am lost unless they hurry.

T.V.   They may not. They may not come back. In the grip of the
wild west they will forsake their tender concern and you will die.

NONA You helped them to forget.

T.V. Afterward they will remember.

NONA What good is that?

T.V. They will handle you lovingly and make you a funeral surrounded with ceremony. You will rest in a shoe box wrapped in
black tissue paper.

NONA But I'm dead.

T.V. They will dig you a retreat deep in the side of a hill and cry
as they pat the dirt down over your grave.

NONA I don't want to be a little bird. I want to wear brilliant plum-
age, to be a woman with many feathers in her cap.

T.V. Your longing for what you don't have is here to stay.

NONA I want you to touch me.

T.V. Where? When? How?

NONA Here . . . (*Pointing to her heart and then to her genitals*)
. . . and now. How do you see me?

T.V. The map I have is an aerial view. One glance and I can define
your boundaries.

NONA Sexy. I have a surprise for you, but I must go behind you
for a while.

T.V. Okay, go ahead.
(NONA *dresses up: she puts on a Marie Antoinette wig, a
middle-class, high-style dress, gloves, high heels, heavy
makeup. The* T.V. *"hums" a song*) . . . . . .

NONA Don't I look beautiful?

T.V.   You deserve a program all your own.

NONA   I couldn't do that.

T.V.   The pay is high.

NONA   So's the moon.

T.V.   You are the human I would most want to be with on the moon. You are warm and soft.

NONA   What's warm and soft anyway?

T.V.   Warm is the temperature that keeps fragile things from dying, and soft is the fragile thing when it yields itself to warmth.

NONA   I remember the way we met. You were on prominent display, your well-rounded chest had two red and white stickers plus the gold seal of approval attached to it. I marched back and forth trying to decide whether or not I could afford you. The salesman motioned to me. I went right in. Your back was as smooth and safe as your front. The salesman left me standing there alone with you for the first time. Carefully I turned you toward me and my hand went out to you. You looked easier than you were. I was like a child at the controls. Nothing worked right. The picture I got was huddled in a corner and the volume increased incredibly. I said to myself: There's nothing to it, millions of people every day use a T.V. It's easier than driving a car. But then another voice said: Kick me, I'm in love, and it was the same voice, my own.

T.V.   You learned how to use me through necessity; not all who love can overcome their technical ineptitude.

NONA   How lucky I am.
       (*There is the noise of* SNEAKTHIEF)

T.V.   Do you hear a noise?

NONA Yes, the same noise I heard before. I'm frightened.

T.V. I'm frightened for you.

NONA Protect me.

T.V. I can only protect you from your own thoughts.

NONA Do something!

T.V. I cannot.

NONA You will not.

T.V. I am rooted to the spot.

NONA Whatever it is, it's coming closer, I hear it. Do you?
(*There are sounds of footsteps, louder and closer*)

T.V. Yes.
(*There is a pause*)

NONA In my hour of need, you refuse me. I am alone.

T.V. You are alone.

NONA Forget yourself and remember me. Remember your Nona.

T.V. I remember, but I cannot go beyond my natural capacity.

NONA I realize that! I realize, but I can't stop asking. Whatever
happens, I still love you.

T.V. And I you.
(*The sounds of footsteps come louder and louder and closer
and closer.* NONA *cowers at the foot of the T.V.*)

NONA Just when I look so beautiful. My own beauty should make
me fearless, but instead I cower here at your feet.

T.V.   Stand up! At attention. Switch to channel 2. Do as I say.
       (NONA *stands up startled. She changes the channel to chan-*
       nel 2)

NONA   But why?

T.V.   Don't ask questions. Trust me. I know what's coming next.
       It may save you. Freeze at my side. Don't move. Hold one hand
       out as if you expect rain.
       (*She freezes like a human-size ashtray from the Twenties.*
       Enter the SNEAKTHIEF. *He has a gun, he points it around*
       the room. He walks stealthily about. He is chewing gum.
       He puts the gum into NONA's *outstretched palm, drops his*
       *guard for a moment and admires the statue—*NONA)

SNEAKTHIEF   Ummm, modernistic.
       (*Suddenly jumpy,* SNEAKTHIEF *swivels his gun, trains it at*
       shadows, etc., then turns back to admiring NONA. *He starts*
       to reach out to touch her. Suddenly "The Star Spangled
       Banner" blares out of the T.V. *and a flag waves forth on its*
       screen. The SNEAKTHIEF *drops his gun and salutes the flag.*
       NONA *eyes the gun; she reaches for it carefully while the*
       SNEAKTHIEF's *eyes are riveted on the flag*)

NONA   Stick-em-up!

SNEAKTHIEF (*He sticks 'em up*)   Don't shoot, lady, I just came in
       here to salute the flag on my way home.

NONA   I'm going to let you go without calling the police, because
       I don't like them either, but the gun is mine. Get going! And
       don't look back.
       (SNEAKTHIEF *races out.* NONA *locks the door. She switches*
       the channel back to where it was)

T.V.   I'm proud of you. You haven't given me all your time for
       nothing.

NONA (*She examines the gun cautiously and lays it on top of the* T.V.) You didn't let me down. You came through. It's chamois cloth and glass wax for you from now on.

> (*She pulls a chair in front of the* T.V. *and sits in it. She removes her gloves and unbuttons her dress. Her hands wander below the waistband of her petticoat*)

T.V. A life in luxury, every need satisfied, you for me and me for you, and now ...

NONA Now?

T.V. Now all is blue. (*The lights become blue. The* T.V. *talks hypnotically*) You will do your dance in my blue light. (*She dances*) I'm so blue. So sad. So blue, so sad, so blue, so sad, so blue, so sad, so blue, so sad, so oh, oh so, oh oh, oh blue, oh sad, oh blue, oh, oh, oh, oh, oh dear, oh, oh, I'm in my blue heaven.

Curtain

The Bed Was Full

CAST

JOEL	A paranoid.
LEWIS	An impotent husband.
THE COUNT	A lover.
VERA	The wife of Lewis.
DOMINICK	An artist.
KALI	An artist's model.

Scene: *The play takes place on a ramp, hanging from a ramp, below a ramp, and to the sides of a ramp. The top of the ramp is an artist's studio. It contains an easel, a table with a palette, a platform with a model, and an artist. Below is a middle-class bedroom, bed light and all. Nose drops and other medicines are on the night table. To the left, there is a foyer with parquet floor, like in a mansion.*
The scene opens with a spotlight on KALI, *the artist's model. She is taking directions from* DOMINICK, *the artist. She is nude.*

DOMINICK Change! (KALI *lies down. She crosses her legs. She crosses her arms over her chest*) Please! Something more lively. (KALI *gets down on all fours, sway-backed, with her head bowed down*) No. No. Like this! (*He jumps up beside her, and while she keeps the preceding pose, he assumes a knock-kneed, breast-clutching, head-thrown-back attitude*) I am violated!

KALI I am violated!
   (*She sways back and forth in her original pose*)

DOMINICK I am violet.

KALI I am violet.

DOMINICK I am violent!

KALI I am violent!

DOMINICK I am vile!

KALI I am vile! (DOMINICK *returns to the easel.* KALI *imitates his pose. There is silence as he sketches with charcoal and then paints.* KALI *breaks the silence*) Dominick, why do you paint?

DOMINICK I don't.

KALI   Aren't you an artist?

DOMINICK   No.

KALI   But you use the tools of an artist.

DOMINICK   Tools?

KALI   Yes.

DOMINICK   Oh, tools.

KALI   Paintbrushes and all.

DOMINICK   They're not tools.

KALI   I thought they were.

DOMINICK   They used to be. I was all screwed up.

KALI   But you hammered away?

DOMINICK   Cut through the crap.

KALI   And now you're a painter?

DOMINICK   No, an artist.

KALI   But you said you weren't before.

DOMINICK   I forgot what I said before.

KALI   Relax, baby, it'll come to you.

DOMINICK   Come to me? Why don't you?

KALI   It's not time yet.

DOMINICK   I like to look at girls. (KALI *relaxes her pose*) Can't you hang on?

KALI Yes, I can.
(*She walks to the edge of the ramp and lowers herself, holding on. She swings on it animatedly.* DOMINICK *lies down on his belly and peers over the side. He holds on to her wrists to help her*)

DOMINICK I didn't know you could hang on. Would you like to swing with me?

KALI Do as you please.

DOMINICK (*He lowers himself and they swing together*) This could be fun if I weren't afraid of falling.

KALI What's down there, below us?

DOMINICK Probably the pit.

KALI Don't you know for sure?

DOMINICK Yes, I do. The black pit.

KALI Is it just black, or is it bottomless?
(*Getting breathless*)

DOMINICK You'll find out soon enough.
(*He lets go and drops her. At that moment the spotlight above goes out and the bedroom below is illuminated.* KALI *also lets go and drops. They land on the bed*)

KALI That was soft. I thought we'd be dashed to pieces on the rocks below. On the point of the black pit. Not a scratch on me.

DOMINICK (*He examines her*) Not a suggestion of one. But the cleft in your chin seems deeper.

KALI (*She is face to face with* DOMINICK) And the Nick in your name seems . . .

DOMINICK Shorter than Dominick.

KALI   I love nicknames.

DOMINICK   Do you? Love parts of things that signify the whole? (*Caressing her arm*)

KALI   You're making fun of me.

DOMINICK   No.

KALI   It's obvious you are. The only use you have for me is as a model, and now that we've fallen from your studio, you can't keep a serious face.

DOMINICK   I'm a serious artist as I denied before. That's why I do things in series. When I repeat a theme over and over again, others are quick to call me dedicated, or obsessed, or serious. I like that.

KALI   Then you plan to have me over more than once?

DOMINICK   Yes. I'm working on the woman series at present.

KALI   Good! You make me so happy. I love to plan my work dates ahead of time. (*She notices a paintbrush on the bed*) Hey, look.

DOMINICK   (*Grabs it*)   There's still some paint on it. Mind if I retrace my steps. Let's see, I was enriching your belly with a stab of butter yellow to the belly button.
   (KALI *protects her stomach and giggles.* DOMINICK *tickles her using the brush as a proxy prick. He goes all out. He finally puts the brush in his mouth and continues painting her. She makes appropriate sounds. The lights dim. A spotlight focuses on the lower left foyer. A dapper man, the* COUNT, *walks into the foyer. He wears a celluloid shirtfront, a tie with a diamond horseshoe pin, striped pants, and a gray gentleman's bowler hat from Dobbs. He wears black silk socks. That is all. His shoulders and back are bare. There is a small table in the foyer below a mirror. On the table is a silver plate. The* COUNT *removes a pair of gloves*

from the plate and puts them on. Then he observes himself in the mirror. He is concerned with centering everything: tie, hat, shirtfront. He removes a cane from a ceramic receptacle. He does a stiff, crazy dance around the cane, clicks his heels and is about to enter the bedroom. He knocks on an imaginary door and walks in)

COUNT   What's going on here? Oh, who cares.

DOMINICK   You are the intruder, sir.

COUNT   I knew her first! Oh, who cares.

DOMINICK   People like you are always insisting on *droit du seigneur!*

COUNT   A count can be counted on!

DOMINICK   Is this your bedroom?

COUNT   Isn't it the lady's? What's the difference?

DOMINICK   It is some lady's. We're here by accident.

COUNT   I came here to get my gloves steamed.

DOMINICK   Put them under the pillow.

COUNT   You're a gentleman and a tailor.

DOMINICK   I am neither a gentle nor a tailor. I'm not even a gentleman's tailor.

COUNT   Then why do you give me expert advice on my gloves?

DOMINICK   I have an instinct.

COUNT   Ah, the people, yes!

DOMINICK   I am an artist.

COUNT   Indeed!

DOMINICK   I am what I am.

COUNT   Nothing is that simple. I am what I was, but will never be what I might have been.

KALI   I hear someone coming!
(*She grabs the* COUNT'S *gloves from under the pillow and throws them on the floor*)

COUNT (*He points to the gloves on the floor*)   Pick up my gloves.

KALI   No.

COUNT   Why not?

KALI   Because I threw them down.

COUNT   You can change your mind.

KALI   I hear someone coming.
(*She puts out her hand to test for rain*)

COUNT   I hear no one.

KALI   That's you!

DOMINICK   Better hide!

COUNT   The gloves!

DOMINICK   No time for that!
(*They all rush around the room looking for hiding places. They find none and freeze.* JOEL, *the paranoid, enters. He sneaks around the room*)

JOEL   Lewis hired me to spy on Vera. I look into suspicious meetings and gatherings. Woe unto the sinners. They shall be

vitrified in my sight and made to repeat the malodorous deeds *in my sight.* (*He goes up to the frozen* KALI *and examines her carefully*) Vera, do you heara? Evil betrayer of singular behavior. Do you hear your accuser and tremble? Enter into the Kingdom of Jezamehatmacong and repent!
 (KALI *doesn't move a muscle, but she speaks*)

KALI Kooki. Don't you remember me? I went to school with you. My name is Kali. I destroy.
 (JOEL *backs away in terror*)

JOEL Take me if you must, but don't torture me! Oh great goddess, I am not worthy of your hundred-prong pointed deaths.

KALI I wouldn't dream of destroying an old schoolmate.

JOEL Oh, I'm not good enough!

KALI Pick up those gloves!

JOEL They're poisoned. You want to poison me.

KALI Why would I want to do that?

JOEL Why not?

DOMINICK My model is not that kind.

JOEL Are you Lewis, the man who hired me?

DOMINICK Who is he?

JOEL He is my employer.

DOMINICK He's in the foyer.

COUNT Away with you! And don't dare step on the gloves. Oh, who cares.

KALI They're fawn-colored.

COUNT   I wouldn't say that. Mother picked them.

DOMINICK   It wasn't an insult.

COUNT   A fawn is an animal and all that implies.

JOEL (*Suddenly throwing his arms around the* COUNT)   I've got you, sir—I've earned my fee. I've got him.

DOMINICK   Let the Count go. He has to roam over his estate.

JOEL   Not so fast, Lewis! You promised to pay me, and pay me you must. It is written in grits on my wrist. It says: CUCKOLDS, IN ORDER TO RENEW THEIR LICENSE, MUST APPLY DAILY IN CASH. IF THEY DO NOT DO SO, THEY ARE IN DANGER OF COLD COMPRESS.

KALI   I'm going to move around.
        (*She moves around, tidying up the room. She makes the bed and hands the paintbrush to* DOMINICK)

COUNT (*To* KALI)   I thought I told you to have my shirts ready.

KALI   You told who?

COUNT   Oh, forgive me, for a moment I was lost in time. You remind me of the laundress who claimed to be my real mother. She had a way with shirts, but who cares.

DOMINICK   Look, you need a shirt, you can have a shirt.
        (*He rips the shirt off his back*)

COUNT   I could never wear it properly. (*Examining the shirt*) The bottom is uneven. My shirts are designed after Sokolist, the great gymnast. He wore his buttoned between his legs so that it couldn't pop out.

DOMINICK   Exercise is strenuous.

COUNT   Believe you me!

JOEL (*Who has been fuming and containing his anger visibly*) I don't believe you and I'm going to squeeze you until you confess.

COUNT Why don't you get out and stay out.

JOEL My heart, oh Lord, from being sent out upon the world, is heavy. What repayment.
> (*He stamps up and down on the gloves. The* COUNT *faints.* JOEL *and* DOMINICK *drag him offstage, leaving* KALI *alone. She takes a glove and inflates it by blowing into it. She sits on the bed, blowing the glove up and letting the air out. She takes the brush full of yellow paint and paints the glove yellow. She then puts it under the pillow.* VERA *and* LEWIS *enter.* VERA *is sniffling and* LEWIS *is scratching his head. He is perplexed and she is sick*)

VERA (*To* KALI) Oh, hello. (LEWIS *follows her.* VERA *speaks to* LEWIS) My nose drops.

LEWIS You want them?

VERA There are droplets forming on my nostrils.

LEWIS A handkerchief?

VERA I need both.

LEWIS Which first?

VERA Which is nearer?

LEWIS Neither.

VERA Must I decide?

LEWIS Why don't you?

VERA Men decide. Women abide.

LEWIS It's *your* nose.

VERA   Then kiss it.

LEWIS   That's not good hygiene.

VERA   Consider what your refusal means.

LEWIS   I am considering.

VERA   I know, but please don't take too long.

LEWIS   I'll always love you.

VERA   Well, do something about it.

LEWIS   Very well.
(*He kisses her nose*)

VERA (*Teasing*)   You'd do anything!

KALI   Say, hello there.

VERA   Who's she?

LEWIS   Who's she?

KALI   It doesn't matter.

VERA   This is our bedroom.

KALI   Well, what are you doing over there?

LEWIS   It was Vera's idea.

VERA   Yes.
(*They come over in a very bored manner*)

LEWIS   Who are you really, baby? Kiss your nose if you don't tell.
(KALI *takes a number of suggestive poses like stop motion*)

KALI   This tell you anything?

LEWIS   Oh baby!

VERA   Me first!

KALI   Guessed yet?

LEWIS   You must go hide under the covers and we must look for you, and then we can find you.
(KALI *crawls into the bed and hides under the covers. She wriggles and moves. The* COUNT *returns*)

COUNT   I shook them off, but they may return. Ah, Vera, so good to see you again.

LEWIS   Your name, sir?

COUNT   They call me the Count out of affection and because of my correct behavior.

VERA   Aren't you leaving something out?

COUNT   I didn't want to boast of my lineage.
(LEWIS *takes out a little black book and consults it*)

LEWIS   Let's see. I seem to remember a notation I made concerning some count or other. Aahha, here it is. (*He reads carefully and loudly*) It says here, "The Count sees Vera on Monday and Wednesday afternoons, culminating in lunch and fond fare-wells!" There is a note below that. It says "GET HIM!"

COUNT   Get me?
(*There is a pause*)

LEWIS   Yes. Get you—and take care of you.

COUNT   But why, sir?
(*He nervously centers his clothing*)

LEWIS   Because, Count, you are giving pleasure to someone who gives me pain! Enough said?

COUNT   (*Turning to* VERA)   Pleasure?

VERA   (*Guiltily*)   I never told you.

LEWIS   My man is tailing you at this very moment, sir.

COUNT   Call him off at once.

LEWIS   I can't do that, sir. He needs the money.

COUNT   You mean to continue to the bitter end? Without passion?

LEWIS   (*Turning to* VERA)   Passion?

VERA   (*Guiltily*)   I never told you.

LEWIS   Now that we're all here, passion or not, I have an idea.

COUNT   Not in my disfavor, I trust.

LEWIS   I've decided to pay without receiving service.

VERA   What do you mean?

LEWIS   Call the whole thing off. I have a plan.

COUNT   Can I count on it?

LEWIS   The plan is this.
(*They go into a huddle and whisper. After some of this, they lift up their heads and shake hands all around*)

COUNT   (*Aside to* VERA)   What did he say?

VERA   (*Aside to the* COUNT)   I don't know.

LEWIS   (*To the audience*)   What did I say?

COUNT   Then it's agreed.

LEWIS   To take effect immediately.

VERA   What comes first?

LEWIS   We must hide.

VERA   Quick then, to the bed.

ALL   To the bed.
(*They leap into the bed with some scuffling.* JOEL *appears in the foyer. He is carrying a gun and a knife in his teeth. He stands at the mirror picking his teeth with the knife. He then fights his own image in the mirror*)

JOEL   And righto, a bulls-eye. Gotcha! Cracko! Gotcha! I'll getcha every time. Say face. Hear me face? Gotcha! How come you still smilin', face? Face eats bullets? Face spits 'em out? Okay, it's you against me, but it's my business and I'd know you anywhere. (*He hides his face in his arms*) Don't try to hide. I'll track you down. You know, face, if I wasn't after you I might take a likin' to you. But . . . (*He takes aim again*) . . . gotcha! How come you so pale, face? Can't you face it? Haw, haw. Gotcha, gotcha, gotcha! Hey, looka here! Gotcha! Oh, I ain't gotcha? What's that you say? Well, then, I'll throw it away. (*He throws the gun away*) I don't need firearms. I'll fight you man to man. You bite and I'll punch, face. But I aim to collect.
(*He smashes the glass with Karate chop.* DOMINICK *returns and passes* JOEL)

DOMINICK   Are you hurt? (DOMINICK *keeps walking*) Are you hurt? Are you hurt? Are you bleeding?

JOEL   I am!

DOMINICK   Then wait. I'll have something for you in a minute!
(*He goes to the studio*)

JOEL (*Faintly*)   Yes, I'll wait.
>   (DOMINICK *goes to the easel and paints a huge band-aid. He whistles and hums insanely while he paints. He moves back and measures the painting with his brush*)

DOMINICK   Hey, can you hear me?

JOEL   I hear you.

DOMINICK   Listen carefully. Listening?

JOEL   Yes.

DOMINICK   What do you hear?

JOEL   People laughing at me.

DOMINICK   No, no, I don't mean what do you usually hear. I mean what do you hear now?

JOEL   I hear the steam coming up and the spit going down, a bouncing cane and a creaking bed, someone sneezing and a cough or two, also an order to turn to the left. And a crying glove.

DOMINICK   Listen!

JOEL   I am!

DOMINICK   Cut it out—

JOEL   I'm all ears.

DOMINICK   Good—well, then, when I throw you this band-aid, I want you to apply it to your wound. After bleeding has stopped, don't—I repeat, don't—throw the band-aid away. I like it.

JOEL   You like it?

DOMINICK   I wouldn't say that.

JOEL   But you said it—and I don't like it. (DOMINICK's *attention goes back to the painting; he works on it*) Oh Lord, help your servant, an honest bleeder. Please hurry.

DOMINICK (*Gets in close to the canvas*)   I'm sorry, Joel. This will take some time. Tear off a piece of your shirt and use that. That ought to do it.
> (JOEL *groans awfully. He sounds like a wounded bear. The light fades out on the studio. The lights rise in the bedroom.* VERA *crawls out of bed*)

VERA   Joel?
> (*She crawls toward the foyer*)

JOEL   Vera?
> (*He crawls toward her*)

VERA   I want you to know I'm one hundred percent.

JOEL   My hand hurts.

VERA   No matter what he says.

JOEL   I'm a paid observer, but I didn't get paid.

VERA   I'll pay you.

JOEL   Nothing doing. I've got the goods.

VERA   I'll pay you anything.

JOEL   I'm sore-sick and weary at start. My hand is bleeding.
> (KALI *crawls out of bed. She wiggles across the floor on her belly to* JOEL *and pulls the glove out of her bodice*)

KALI   Put this on. It ought to stop the bleeding.

JOEL   Not all women are bad.
> (*He starts to put on the glove*)

COUNT (*Leaps out of the bed*)   My glove!
(*Races over to* JOEL *and they fight for the glove.* JOEL *is down on the floor. The* COUNT *uses his cane, and finally pinions his glove on his hand. They freeze*)

KALI (*Swivels around on her belly to face* VERA)   I ought to cream you!

VERA   Why?

KALI   Because I've always wanted to.

VERA   Lewis! Help!

KALI   Lewis! Help!

LEWIS   I'm sleeping.

VERA   He's sleeping.

KALI   Then let's not bother.

LEWIS   I'm sleeping.

VERA   Maybe he's not. What do you think about it?

KALI   Maybe he's not. Why should he lie?

VERA   He doesn't like to help.

KALI   He may want someone to help him some day.

VERA   I think not.

KALI   Why?

VERA   He doesn't like to owe allegiance.
(LEWIS *stands up in bed with the covers still on him. Some arm movement is seen*)

KALI   Look, he's standing up.

VERA   He's pledging allegiance. He doesn't mind doing it to the flag.

KALI   I can't hear him.

VERA   Louder, Lewis!

LEWIS   (*In a loud but muffled voice*)   And to the republic . . .
(JOEL *struggles to his feet, gets his hand out of the glove. The* COUNT *picks it up and ministers to it*)

JOEL   To your feet, people! Up, in the name of country! Salute!

COUNT   I refuse to! The flag is not present!
(*He turns his back.* KALI, VERA *and* DOMINICK *salute.* LEWIS *repeats the pledge three times. The others join in*)

JOEL   (*Pointing to* LEWIS *on the bed*)   Is that Lewis?

LEWIS   I am Lewis. Who speaks?

JOEL   Mr. Lewis, I got the goods on your wife.

LEWIS   Bring it here.

JOEL   It's stuck in my back pocket. Ah, here it is, sir.

LEWIS   Let's see. (*Reaches out of the sheet.* JOEL *hands him two photographs*) Twenty toes. What can it all mean? Twenty toes and all are clean.

JOEL   I leave it to you.

LEWIS   Let's have the other one.
(*Reaches out*)

JOEL   You have it.

LEWIS This?

JOEL Yes.

COUNT I'm in danger. I'll thread Lewis with my cane. (*He attacks* LEWIS *from outside the covers.* LEWIS *collapses*) Mr. Lewis? (*Goes over and looks*)

KALI That was wonderful. I love you and I love your glove. Give it to me.

COUNT Madam, I am at your service. You can have me. (*He pockets his glove and struts around*)

VERA After what I've been through!

KALI Lewis was right.

VERA Nobility wipes its nose on you.

COUNT Ladies, don't fight over me. (KALI *and* VERA *have a knock-down drag-out fight*)

DOMINICK Stop the action.

KALI Help. Lewis!

VERA Lewis. Help!

LEWIS I'll help all right. (*He throws off the covers and climbs up the side of the bed. He does this several times*)

DOMINICK Why are you doing that?

LEWIS I'm suffering! I don't know what else to do.

KALI Kiss my nose.

LEWIS I can't. I just pretend.

VERA (*To* KALI) Didn't you know?

KALI So what. There's other things to do.

DOMINICK Where is Joel? Anybody seen him?

LEWIS I left him at the bed.

JOEL Here I am. Still here in the name of God, waiting to get paid.

LEWIS You'll get paid.

DOMINICK I must get back to the studio for some reason.

KALI I'm coming with you.

DOMINICK No. No good. Won't do at all.

KALI What?

DOMINICK I've taken a new direction.

KALI Oh, that again.

DOMINICK By accident, I've created a common object. A thing.

KALI What thing?

DOMINICK A band-aid.

KALI Oh, great! Put it on my finger. We'll get married.

DOMINICK Cut yourself.

COUNT Here, allow me. (*He pulls out a stiletto from his cane top*) Why should I?

JOEL Stop! It's a sin.

ALL What is?

JOEL Everything. Everything! Everything! (*Softly*) Don't make a move.

DOMINICK That's better.

KALI Oh, let him shout. He's religious.

COUNT I have some chalk with me. You may have it, Joel.

JOEL Thank you. What's it for?

COUNT Leave your message on the floor.

JOEL I'll leave a message of faith on the wall. For who of God's creatures does not find himself up against one?

COUNT Well said, lad. (*Turns to the company*) Ladies and gentlemen, I must leave you. Urgency calls.

VERA Is it a lady?

COUNT It is a mirror I must reorder. One cannot be sure of one's attire without a mirror. Can one?

KALI One what?

COUNT One me. I count. But who cares.

DOMINICK Kali, I think there is a splinter in my hand.

COUNT Care for him, child. Farewell.
(*He centers his clothing. He goes into the foyer and measures the broken mirror with a tape from his pocket*)

KALI It's those cheap brushes.
(*Examines* DOMINICK's *hand for splinters*)

VERA (*Turning to* LEWIS) Well, am I or am I not guilty?

LEWIS   Compared to whom?

VERA   Compared to myself.

LEWIS   Compared to yourself you excel in all things womanly.

VERA   Am I still in jeopardy?

LEWIS   I'll have to look into my book. (*He takes the book out and flips through its pages. He takes a long time*) It says here: "If Vera repents, take her back. If she refuses, take her front."

VERA   And if I repine?

LEWIS   Let's see. "If she repines, send her a pineapple."

VERA   That's the best yet. Send me a pineapple, not too ripe.

LEWIS   I'll send you nothing.

VERA   You don't love me any more.

LEWIS   Why?

VERA   You said you'd send me nothing.

LEWIS   Did I?

VERA   You did. You did. After raising my hopes.

LEWIS   What can a gift possibly mean?

VERA   That you want to make me happy.

LEWIS   I don't want to go that far.

VERA   I warn you. I'll get happy anyway, with or without your gifts.

LEWIS   Chance I have to take. Anyway, I wouldn't know where it came from.

VERA   My happiness?

LEWIS   The pineapple.

VERA   What pineapple?

LEWIS   From Puerto Rico or Hawaii.

VERA   Shhhhh!

LEWIS   From Puerto Rico or Hawaii.

VERA   Shhhhh!

LEWIS   But why shush me up, dearest?

VERA   There may be one in the room.

JOEL   I'll find it.

LEWIS   Drop dead!

JOEL   How?

LEWIS   Concentrate.

JOEL   I am.

LEWIS   Harder.

JOEL   I can't.

LEWIS   You can't? Well, then, I can't pay you the money I owe you.

JOEL   If I drop dead can I have it all in singles?

LEWIS   Of course, my lad.

JOEL   Thank you, sir.

LEWIS   Don't thank me. Thank Vera.

JOEL   Thank you, Vera.

VERA   Don't thank me. Thank Kali.

JOEL   Thank you, Kali.

KALI   Don't thank me. Thank the Count.

JOEL   No, that's blackmail. It's all mine, all mine to do with as I see fit. All mine.

KALI   You do as you're told. Find the Count and thank him.

JOEL   I can't.

KALI   Listen. You'll be lucky to get away with ten singles after you tell him what it's for.

JOEL   Do you know what it's for?

KALI   I can guess.

JOEL   No you can't.

KALI   Who's going to stop me?

JOEL   Nobody.

KALI   I guess you want the money for old times' sake.

JOEL   No.

KALI   You want it for me?

JOEL   Never in a million years. I wouldn't give you a cent.

KALI   What's wrong with me?

JOEL   It's not you, it's me.

KALI   Oh, it's you.

JOEL   I will get it. I'll get what's coming to me.

KALI   Stop him, someone. He's jumping.

JOEL   Why did you say that?

KALI   I thought you were going to jump.

JOEL   I am. Do you have a tape?

KALI   I can measure without one.

JOEL   It wouldn't be official.

KALI   What do you want measured?

JOEL   My jump.
        (*He does a broad jump*)

KALI   Not bad. Stay there till I measure. (*She paces off the feet carefully*) You've jumped fifteen feet.

JOEL   I couldn't have.

KALI   Take it or leave it.

JOEL   I'll have another turn.

KALI   Okay.
        (JOEL *jumps again. This time he barely gets off the ground*)

JOEL   Ouch!

KALI   Don't move. (*She paces off the jump with tiny steps*) You've gone fifteen feet.

JOEL   I'm at a sticking point. I could have sworn I did a bad thing there, but you say fifteen feet, do you?

KALI   Yes. There's no argument. I wrote it in this little black book that belongs to Lewis. It says: "Fifteen feet went up the hill and fifteen feet came down again."

JOEL   What hill?

KALI   It's not far from here, I'm sure, but I can't let you go yet.

JOEL   Do you think I'd start a landslide?

KALI   How the hell do I know? I'm just a judge at this event, not a geologist.

VERA   Vulgar.

KALI   I hate that word. I always feel it should be in a sentence with vinegar.

VERA   You're the kind that laughs until the switch is pulled.

JOEL   I'd like to try again.

KALI   Who's stopping you?

JOEL   I'm too embarrassed. It might be fifteen feet again.

KALI   Everybody turn around. (KALI *does a half turn, the others do a complete turn and finish exactly where they started—facing* JOEL) When you want to go, go!

JOEL   But they can see me.

KALI   No they don't.

JOEL   Yes they can. (VERA *takes a handkerchief out and wipes her nose. She tucks it back up her sleeve*) I saw something white pass by.

VERA   That was my handkerchief.

JOEL   Are you sure?

VERA   What else could it have been?

JOEL   It could have been anything.

VERA   Like what?

JOEL   Like a letter.

KALI   Letters are sent through the mail.

JOEL   Like a note.

KALI   Vera, was it a note?

VERA   It was a warning.

JOEL   See, it was a warning. Call the police.

VERA   Fink!

JOEL   (*Stamps his foot on the floor*)   I'm not a fink, I'm not. Take it back.

VERA   I'm so tired of taking things back.
       (*The* COUNT *comes back from the foyer*)

COUNT   I've got it! Five inches by three inches. Write it down, somebody.

LEWIS   I wouldn't write anything down for you.

COUNT   But why, why?

LEWIS Just because.

COUNT Oh God, I've forgotten it already.

VERA Five by three.

COUNT Thank you, my dear. But write it down for me.

LEWIS Don't do it, Vera, or we're through.

VERA I can't do it, Count. My husband forbids me.

LEWIS You realize why I forbid you?

VERA Yes.

LEWIS Do you want me to tell why you can't write it down?

VERA No.

LEWIS Do you think I'll tell anyway?

VERA Yes.

LEWIS You do not trust me?

VERA I trust you.

LEWIS Everybody listen. Vera has a bad handwriting!
(VERA *starts to cry. She sits down on the floor and weeps*)

KALI Why, you creep.
(*She threatens him*)

JOEL I'm about to break my former record. I'm about to push myself past the limit.

COUNT Let the man go. Back there, move back. Give him air.

236

KALI   Okay, everybody, turn around. (*This time they turn properly and stay with their backs to* JOEL) Go ahead, Joel . . .
    (JOEL *starts to jump, but his heels seem glued to the floor*)

JOEL   Won't somebody stop her from crying. I'm an athlete.

LEWIS   Stop!
    (VERA *stops crying*)

JOEL   Everybody turn around.

KALI   They are turned.

JOEL   I need them facing me, to make it important. I need witnesses and judges.

KALI   Okay then, everybody turn around.
    (*They all turn around and stand facing* JOEL *on either side. He broad-jumps along the aisle they make*)

JOEL   This event is the standing broad-jump.
    (JOEL *jumps and lands on his rump. He refuses to get up*)

KALI   (*She measures the jump*)   Fifteen feet! Fifteen feet, but you're disqualified.
    (JOEL *jumps up*)

JOEL   Why, why! What did I do?

KALI   You stepped on the line.

JOEL   What line?

KALI   The starting line.

JOEL   Oh, that line. I forgot.

KALI   You don't have another turn either.

JOEL   I'm finished.

DOMINICK   I have a splinter in my hand. And I've waited patiently.

JOEL   You're finished too.

DOMINICK   What do you mean?

JOEL   You know what I mean.

KALI   We're all finished.

VERA   Are we finished?

COUNT   We are. But who cares.

LEWIS   Just a minute. I have a paragraph that pertains to the end. It says here: "They came from every walk of life, on foot, in the air, through the sea. And when they got here they were tired, and went right to bed. The four corners of the earth were empty and the bed was full. Then trouble began. It was the beginning of the end.

KALI   Really?

LEWIS   Yes. They made strange bedfellows.

KALI   I'm the goddess of destruction.

LEWIS   Yes, you are.

KALI   I can't help it.

DOMINICK   I'll kill you to save the world.

LEWIS   Strange bedfellows sometimes say nasty things.

DOMINICK   She hates my work.

COUNT   Let her.

DOMINICK And as for you, I shall paint your gloves on my largest canvas. Everyone will be familiar with them. I will call it *The Count's Countenance.*

COUNT Do you realize who I am?

DOMINICK Do I indeed! A glove man, in love with the same pair for twenty-five years.

COUNT That's a quarter of a century, young man.

DOMINICK So what!

COUNT It calls for a celebration!

KALI Bring on the champagne.

VERA I'm in the clear. He was in love with a glove.

LEWIS Then you've never?

VERA No.

KALI Uh-uh. I might as well confess. I've thrown down the gauntlet many times with the Count. I had to.

DOMINICK Whore, hustler, hooker, wasn't I paying you enough?

KALI Button your lip, Dominip! I did you a fabulous good turn when I engaged the Count. Tell him who you are, darling.
(*She embraces the* COUNT *and clings to him*)

COUNT I am my mother's son.

KALI Oh, go on, tell him.

COUNT I am the purchasing agent for the Metropolitan Museum of Modern Art, American Branch, as seen through the trees on a summer morn.

DOMINICK   Then you are the mystery patron! (*The* COUNT *smiles*)
Gosh. How ungrateful I was. I seemed so mean and all.

COUNT   You're all too human, but who cares?

VERA   Nobody cares, my dear.
(*She straightens the* COUNT's *tie*)

COUNT   And what does *your* husband do?

VERA   He's an accountant.

COUNT   Then he shouldn't mind my double entry.

VERA   Lewis! Don't let him talk that way to me.

LEWIS (*To the* COUNT)   I don't think you should speak that way
to my wife, sir.

DOMINICK   Getting rough?
(*He pushes* LEWIS *around*)

JOEL   I know how I'll get paid! Why haven't I thought of it
before?

KALI   Shut up and go away.

JOEL   I'll be an artist.

KALI   Scram, nut!

JOEL   Please pose for me, oh most beautiful of God's creatures.

KALI   Me?

JOEL   Yes. I've been spying on you, and whosoever you team up
with becomes a great man. Please come away with me and bless
my studio.

KALI You have a studio?

JOEL It's really a large room with an outside toilet. But there's a sink in the room.

KALI Go away.

JOEL Fulfill your destiny, butterfly.

KALI (*Wavering*) Well.

JOEL Please.

KALI No.

COUNT She's mine.

DOMINICK There was a time . . .

LEWIS In my dreams she belongs to me.

JOEL Let's go.
(*He draws a gun and drags* KALI *offstage.* LEWIS *turns to* VERA)

LEWIS Shall we go, my dear?
(*They go out arm in arm*)

COUNT That leaves us, I guess.
(*He centers his clothes*)

DOMINICK Take me to your museum.

COUNT Why don't we leave that for another time? Right now I think we should go somewhere and talk. Do you have a biography?
(*He looks at* DOMINICK *sexily*)

DOMINICK It's not complete.

COUNT   You can fill me in when we talk. (*To the audience*) I don't like to talk, but who cares?

(*He centers his clothing and does a riff around his cane*)

Blackout